Anonymous

Select orations, and other important papers, relative to the Swedish Academy

Anonymous

Select orations, and other important papers, relative to the Swedish Academy

ISBN/EAN: 9783337728588

Printed in Europe, USA, Canada, Australia, Japan

Cover: Foto ©ninafisch / pixelio.de

More available books at **www.hansebooks.com**

SELECT ORATIONS,

AND OTHER

IMPORTANT PAPERS,

RELATIVE TO THE SWEDISH ACADEMY.

FOUNDED

BY HIS PRESENT MAJESTY

GUSTAVUS III.

MARCH 20TH, 1786.

TRANSLATED FROM THE SWEDISH LANGUAGE

BY

N. G. AGANDE.

LONDON:
PRINTED BY T. DAVISON, FLEET-STREET;
FOR J. JOHNSON, ST. PAUL'S CHURCH-YARD.
M,DCC,XCII.

TABLE of CONTENTS.

FRONTISPIECE emblematical of the Inftitution of the SWEDISH Academy on the 20th of March, 1786.

1. EXPLANATION of the Frontifpiece.

2. INAUGURAL Oration, delivered by the KING in the SWEDISH Academy, March 20, 1786.

3. A DISCOURSE delivered in the SWEDISH Academy on Dec. 20, 1786, by Mr. de ROSENSTEIN, perpetual Secretary, &c.

4. DISCOURSE delivered by Mr. SIÖBERG on his Admiffion to the SWEDISH Academy, May 13, 1787.

5. CURSORY Remarks on Tafte and the Belles Lettres, read to the SWEDISH Academy, Dec. 20, 1787, by Mr. de ROSENSTEIN, perpetual Secretary, &c.

6. DISCOURSE delivered by the Count OXENSTIERNA, &c. March 20, 1786.

EXPLANATION OF THE FRONTISPIECE.

THE lustre of the Fine Arts, which succeffively illuminates the different parts of the world, is reprefented by that Vivid Radiance, with which in northern climates, the evening fky, juft at the fetting of the Sun, is beautifully decorated.

A LOFTY range of Rude Mountains covered with Ice and Snow, allude to the State of SWEDEN, before the introduction of the Arts and Sciences. On the Summit of one of thefe Mountains APOLLO reclines. His Lyre, fufpended from his fhoulders, refts upon the Rock. The place confeffes the prefence of the GOD, and the Ice and Snow are feen to melt away. This Deity, in the act of taking off his Mafk, difcovers the refpected Countenance of GUSTAVUS III.

REVIVING as at the return of fpring after a fevere winter, the Shrubs appear in a ftate of vegetation; and difplay the effect of that genial warmth, which is derived from the influence of the God of day.

THE

EXPLANATION of the FRONTISPIECE.

The sceptred Apollo points to a large Temple situated at a distance. In the frieze of this edifice are exhibited those insignia which characterize the different Academies at Stockholm: that of the Sciences; that of the Belles Lettres, History, and Antiquities; that of Painting, Sculpture and Architecture; that of Music; all of which have been embellished by the munificence of Gustavus III.

The front displays a Serpent, the emblem of Eternity; and exhibits the motto of the Swedish Academy: " To Genius and Taste."

In the foreground appear several Groups of Spectators, representing the inhabitants of the North. Some of them behold with admiration the Sanctuary of Science, while others with gratitude direct their attention towards the august Monarch, who is at once the honour and the patron of the Arts. Under their feet they trample beds of Thistles, an emblem of the ignorance of former ages.

Neque quemquam magis decet, vel meliora scire, vel plura quam PRINCIPEM, cujus doctrina omnibus potest prodesse subjectis.

Veget.

AN ORATION,

DELIVERED BY HIS SACRED MAJESTY

GUSTAVUS III.

ON THE FOUNDATION OF THE

SWEDISH ACADEMY,

MARCH 20, 1786.

AN ORATION

BY

GUSTAVUS III.

To promote the welfare of my kingdom, has ever been my first object; to increase the glory of the Swedish name, my warmest wish. The fame of our country has long been diffused throughout Europe by our victorious arms: but, whilst its splendor has dazzled our eyes, it has too frequently excited sorrow in our hearts. Another species of fame is still reserved for our attainment, that which attends upon Literature and the the cultivation of the Liberal Arts — a fame which bids defiance to the ravages of time, and despises the transient celebrity of conquest. This is an excellence, however, which can only be acquired in seasons of public tranquillity. The spark of genius is indeed not unfrequently elicited by the rude conflicts of the warring elements; but in seasons of tumult and desolation, it is speedily smothered and expires. Extinguished by the tempests of war, the sacred embers of genius must be fostered into flame by the gentle zephyr of peace. While, however, the blessing of peace contributes to the prosperity and happiness of a state, still it must be confessed that it too frequently creates in the minds of men a barbarous indolence, and damps the ardour of that genius, which, under more favourable circumstances, would have enlightened and adorned the country in which it was produced. Such indeed is the nature of man, that he can be animated only by action, and must have strong motives to excite his mental powers. A state of tranquillity, so essential to human happiness, has a wonderful tendency to enervate the understanding, unless mankind are impelled to utility by the most powerful motives, and are prevented by the prospect of fame from sinking into a lethargic slumber, equally dangerous to individuals and to the community at large.

THAT emulation and energy, which are excited by the sciences and literature, are, during a season of tranquillity, the only means of preserving in the mind that ardour which prompts men to serve their country, and in every threatening danger to rescue it from ruin.

UNLESS, however, our language be cultivated in foreign countries, the merit of the best compositions will be little known; nor, until it be reduced

duced to the œconomy of settled laws, is such a cultivation possible. Without good writers, a language will never rise into estimation; and, without established rules, it cannot be written with propriety.

For the accomplishment of these important purposes, I have this day founded an institution; and I appoint you, gentlemen, to establish laws for the construction of the Swedish language, and to raise to perfection that structure, of which I have at this time only laid the basis.

To effect this, it is requisite that science, genius, learning, and taste, should all concur: but these are seldom united in one person. It became necessary, therefore, to establish a society, composed of members who felt an ardent attachment to polite literature, and who had devoted their lives to its cultivation; of men who, by extensive learning, had formed their judgments on the knowledge of ages; men who, in the highest offices of state, or in the common intercourse of social life, had from their infancy refined their taste, by that accuracy which their high offices require, and by the variety of characters which they have had an opportunity of examining; men who, of necessity, must attend to precision of language, to an accurate choice of words, and who, of course, must acquire that delicacy of sentiment, which appropriates to each term its exact meaning, and fixes the limits to which in its application it ought to be confined.

If such a society can accomplish the great object which I have in view, what may we not expect from the institution which I now establish,

lish, composed, as it is, of members so respectable? I esteem it no trivial glory, that, under my reign, so many noblemen of distinction, and men of eminence in the world of letters, have concurred in an enterprise, which promises to reflect so much honour on the Swedish language, and from which they will one day derive immortal fame. What may not the present age expect from an institution, illuminated in its origin by such a constellation of genius? But how much more important is the judgment of posterity? that posterity for whom you are to exert your talents; who, neither dazzled by the false glare of partial commendation, nor deceived by the cloud of contemporary censure, will see, with a distinguishing eye, the real value of each man's abilities; of that posterity, who, in the annals of the academy, will perceive the same names, which the records of the kingdom have consigned to the page of history; who will observe, that the first * of the Swedish senators, the first among the founders of a learned society, is also the first member of this academy—a place which he occupies not only as an admirer of the liberal arts, but as a most accurate judge of every thing connected with taste and polite literature.

Next to him may justly be mentioned, as a deserving member of a learned society, a senator † now absent, who, animated in the career of

---

* The senator Count Hopken, one of the first founders of the Academy of Sciences at Stockholm in 1739, and first member of that of the Belles Lettres when instituted in 1753.

† The senator Count C. F. Scheffer.

learning

learning by that patriotic ardour which illuſtrates every action of his life, unites to the beauty of ſtyle the utmoſt delicacy of taſte, and upon whoſe talents I ſhould ſtill further enlarge, did I not apprehend that the tribute of gratitude, which truth demands at my hands, would be thought a ſtudied encomium upon him, to whom I am indebted for my education.

To unite, in an advanced age, the moſt ſocial temper of mind and the moſt elegant taſte for compoſition, with the direction of a political department, which requires more induſtry than abilities, more accuracy than genius—a department which appears even calculated to extinguiſh theſe qualities, is a ſingular circumſtance, a circumſtance which proves more powerfully than any encomium, how much that ſenator *, to whom I now allude, is likely to ornament and inſtruct the academy. The effects of his genius, preſerved in the tranſactions of the kingdom, have already procured him a reputation, which, however, he is deſirous of ſharing with this ſociety.

No perſon, however, can have a better title to become a member of an inſtitution, deſtined to purify the Swediſh language, than a nobleman † who has ſo frequently addreſſed the general aſſemblies of the kingdom; who, with ſo elegant an arrangement, ſo luminous a perſpicuity, and ſo irreſiſtible an energy, has ſo often delivered his ſentiments to his

* The ſenator Count HERMANSSON, who was twice Preſident of the Exchequer.
† The ſenator and field-marſhal Count A. FERSEN, who has been three times Speaker to the Diet.

fellow-citizens. You revive, my worthy nobles, those times of ancient Rome, when the most distinguished citizens united the culture of the liberal arts with the highest offices in the republic; when, with the same voice with which they enforced the interest of their country, and with the same hand that signed the decrees of the senate, they enlightened their fellow-citizens, and not only adorned their language by the elegance of their own writings, but established its permanency on the certain foundation of unerring rules. What, indeed, is the purity of a language? What is the beauty of style? Is it not the expressing of clear thoughts in concise, strong, and perspicuous terms, to which ambiguous meanings cannot be assigned, and which exhibit sentiments in the same correct form in which they rise upon the mind? Does not every man perceive the advantage which the public would derive from this accuracy, in whatever most essentially regards the interest and peace of society? If treaties, conventions, and laws, were expressed in fixed, indisputable, and acknowledged terms, they would be no longer exposed to that obscurity, that doubt, those perpetual explanations, which often, to illustrate an obscure passage, entirely alter the wisest ordinances; and how many examples have we of the inconveniences which such explanations introduce! Our own annals will sufficiently exemplify this assertion.

WITH you, my worthy nobles, those gentlemen are this day united, who have both enriched and embellished the Swedish language; and in the midst of an assembly, whose talents are consecrated to the eulogy of the national heroes and benefactors, and whose anniversary festival is to
be

AN ORATION BY GUSTAVUS III.

be celebrated on the birth-day of the great GUSTAVUS-ADOLPHUS, how can that man be forgotten, whose name will ever be inseparably united with that of the illustrious hero, whose death he has with such pathetic elegance lamented? a poet *, who combines the truest accuracy of taste, with those graces of style, which his natural sensibility, his well-known probity, and his amiable talents for conversation, have enabled him to acquire.

THAT accomplished scholar †, who adorns with such elevated language those papers which issue from that office of the state which is under his administration, and who, in obedience to my commands, has written, with such truth and eloquence, the life of an aged and illustrious knight, who, commencing his career of glory under the ALEXANDER of of the North, grew grey, and ended his days in my court: such an author has certainly the best claim to a distinguished seat in a society, the object of which is eloquence.

THE poet ‡, who, in so animated a strain, has celebrated the victories of CHARLES-GUSTAVUS; whose writings, for more than twenty years,

---

* The senator Count T. G. OXENSTIERNA, First Lord of the Bedchamber to his Majesty; Grand Master of her Majesty's Household; author of an Ode on the death of GUSTAVUS-ADOLPHUS, and of many other pieces of great merit.

† Mr. de SCHRÖDERHEIM, Secretary of State; author of an Eulogy on Count LIE-VEN, Secretary and Marshal of the kingdom.

‡ Count G. F. GYLLENBORG, author of an Epic Poem entitled *The March over the Bält*, of *The Man-Hater*, and many other valuable works.

C   have

have adorned the Swedish language; by becoming a member of this society, certainly confers upon it more honour than he receives.

THE interest of the academy could not have been better consulted, than by intrusting it to his care, who is the sacred depository * of my future hope, and that of the nation; whose agreeable manner of communicating knowledge, whose extensive learning, and acquaintance with elegant literature, have gained him the esteem of foreigners, and have introduced him to that high confidential station which he now occupies.

To write history with truth and perspicuity, requires courage as well as learning; to render it elegant and useful, requires intelligence, philosophy, and taste. How extensive then are the claims of that member †, and what assistance may we not expect from his superior talents, who has already so far promoted the object for which the academy is instituted?

On this occasion, it is impossible to forget those two poets; of whom, the one ‡ has, with so much elegance, introduced the heroes of HOMER and EURIPIDES on the Swedish stage, and who has expressed, with such

---

* Mr. de ROSENSTEIN, Counsellor to the Grand Council of the Royal Chancery, tutor to the Prince Royal.

† Mr. de BOTIN, Counsellor to the Exchequer; author of a work entitled *A Sketch of the History of the Swedish Nation*; and of another *On the Swedish Language, considered with regard to Conversation and Writing*.

‡ Mr. ADLERBETH, Secretary to the King; author of the Tragedy of *Iphigenia in Aulis*, with choruses, performed in 1776; and of the Opera of *Cora and Alonzo*, represented in 1782.

exquisite

exquisite sensibility, the passion of CORA and ALONZO; the other *, who, with all the energy of poetry, has invoked from the grave, if we may be allowed the expression, the patriotic spirit of GUSTAVUS VASA, has exhibited that illustrious hero, who more than two centuries ago rescued our ancestors from the galling yoke of civil and religious bondage, and brought him before our eyes, once more to receive the glad homage of the Swedish people.

Two respectable prelates, whom I have not the satisfaction of seeing upon this occasion, have a just claim to be ranked amongst the members of this assembly; the one †, at a period when history was a mere chronicle, has recorded, in a manly style, the exalted actions of GUSTAVUS ERICSON, and vindicated his son from the unjust aspersions with which his memory was stained; the other has ‡, with all the graces of eloquence, inculcated divine truth, and, by fulfilling, in the most exemplary manner, the duties of his important station, has essentially improved the language, and refined the taste of the nation.

FROM writers thus eminent, the Swedish language may expect a new and glorious æra. The object which we have in view, is not unworthy

---

* Mr. KELLGREN, private Secretary to the King, and author of the Lyric Tragedy of *Gustavus Vasa*, performed in 1786, with great success.

† Dr. CELSIUS, Bishop of Lund, author of *The Histories of Gustavus I.* and *of Eric XIV.*

‡ Dr. VINGARD, Bishop of Gothenburgh, no less celebrated for his Sermons on various subjects, than for his Funeral Oration on the Death of the late Queen Dowager.

the attention of thofe, who have facrificed the whole of their time to the higheft offices of the ftate. Nor am I deftitute of other arguments, to juftify an inftitution, which in itfelf poffeffes the utmoft utility. I am not unconfcious that there are fome perfons, who regard literature and the liberal arts as deftitute of utility, as a fpecies of luxury, which, being calculated only for the amufement of an effeminate people, ought to be banifhed from a manly and martial nation. Yet, what are the rewards to which the valiant afpire, if not to an immortal reputation? What probability is there that the deferving foldier would facrifice his eafe, and endure the invidious flander of his contemporaries, were he not fupported by the hope, that an enlightened pofterity would render juftice to his fame? But how could this expectation be indulged, if no men of genius exifted, to deliver down to futurity the eulogy of heroes? And, to an elegant mind, what duty more delightful, what occupation more worthy the leifure of the ftatefman, than to revive the memory of illuftrious patriots? Who can more truly eftimate the merit of human actions, and more juftly reprefent them, than they, who, from their infancy, have ftudied purity of language; or than they, who, from a long acquaintance with the higheft offices of ftate, have gained an intimate knowledge of the art of government?

To honour the memory of great characters, is to exhort their defcendants to refemble them; it is to proclaim — Warriors, judges, ftatefmen, citizens! you who have inherited the names of heroes, or have fucceeded to their rank, behold the tribute of gratitude which they receive from pofterity, and render yourfelves, if poffible, worthy of equal honours:
your

your names muſt appear before the tribunal of future ages; let not their luſtre be obſcured through your degeneracy; it is in your power to render them equally renowned.

Such is the important truſt which I now commit to your care. I have endeavoured to diſcharge my duty: it remains for you to fulfil yours. While you contemplate with attention the records of paſt ages, you will take care to keep in view the judgment of the future; and this conſideration will not a little enable you to deſerve their applauſe.

AN ORATION,

DELIVERED BEFORE THE SWEDISH ACADEMY,

ON THE TWENTIETH DAY OF DECEMBER 1786, THE ANNIVERSARY
OF THE BIRTH-DAY OF

GUSTAVUS-ADOLPHUS,

BY

M. DE ROSENSTEIN,

COUNSELLOR TO THE GRAND COUNCIL OF THE ROYAL CHANCERY, TUTOR TO
HIS R. H. THE PRINCE ROYAL OF SWEDEN, PERPETUAL SECRETARY
TO THE SWEDISH ACADEMY, MEMBER OF THE ROYAL
ACADEMY OF THE BELLES LETTRES, HISTORY,
AND ANTIQUITIES, KNIGHT OF THE
POLAR STAR.

AN

ORATION

BY

M. DE ROSENSTEIN.

GENTLEMEN,

THIS day the Academy, for the first time, celebrates a festival, which, annually renovated, will annually present its enquires and decisions to a respectable public, whose judgment it esteems, and whose approbation it is ambitious of obtaining. Had the choice been left to us, gratitude without doubt would have induced us to have selected, as the epocha of our anniversary, the day on which the academy was instituted. We should by that means have enjoyed a desirable and well-chosen opportunity of presenting those oblations of veneration and love which we owe to our auguſt founder. But, ſince the commemoration of this inſtitution has been confided, as well as the memory of many other great events, to the profound, though ſilent ſentiments of grateful hearts; ſince it is committed to the tardy, but juſt and durable teſtimony of hiſtory, whoſe voice will ſpeak to the lateſt poſterity, it is to be preſumed that we ſhall not be refuſed the privilege of manifeſting the gratitude, veneration, and pleaſure, which animate our breaſts, in beholding the æra of the foundation of this academy connected with one of the moſt happy and memorable days in the annals of our country, the day which gave birth to GUSTAVUS-ADOLPHUS. If, without incurring the reproach of ſelf-complacency, we may be allowed to believe that an eſtabliſhment, deſtined to cultivate a language of heroes, to excite the poet and the orator to immortalize the proofs of Swediſh valour, to keep alive among us a taſte for the ſublime, the beautiful, the pathetic, the noble, and the natural; if we ought to believe that ſuch an inſtitution is in ſome degree connected with the glory of our country, what name could more forcibly animate us to perſevere in the purſuit of this grand object than that of GUSTAVUS-ADOLPHUS? a hero who, among all nations, in all countries and ages, ſuperior to the fluctuation of opinion, will preſerve an everlaſting claim to the admiration of mankind, and reflect on Sweden the moſt brilliant reputation. Where is the man, indeed, whoſe title to immortal fame was ever better founded than that of the heroic GUSTAVUS-ADOLPHUS?—A monarch mighty among kings: though receiving a kingdom, diſtracted by diſſenſions, and ſurrounded by enemies, he tranſmitted it to his ſucceſſors in perfect peace, aggrandized by his efforts,

dreaded

dreaded by the neighbouring potentates, and respected throughout all Europe—A monarch mighty among heroes; not for having, like ordinary warriors, encountered dangers, triumphed over opposition, and surmounted difficulties, but because he loved justice, because his prudence was not lulled to security by success, because he was never intoxicated by prosperity, because his exalted spirit never submitted to the slavery of his passions, and because his exploits ended in restoring to the rights of mankind two of the most powerful empires on the face of the earth. In addition to this, he possesses a reputation peculiar to himself; a reputation which will last, even though at some remote period of time, amid the probable revolutions in the fate of empires, future generations should look with less respect on those events which have established a balance between the powers of Europe. He has the fairest claim to the honour of *invention*, of having given a new face to the art of war, and of ranking in the number of his pupils all the great commanders which this quarter of the globe has produced since that period. Is it necessary to add, that humanity, which shudders at the very name of war, cannot raise her voice to impeach the fame of a hero, whose example never instructed mankind to add to the perils and destruction unavoidable in war; that unjustifiable cruelty of conduct, which the want of feeling and a ferocious self-interest too frequently produce?

THE remembrance of this day has drawn me into a subject much beyond my feeble powers: but before I quit it, I must beg leave to improve the opportunity, by expressing a fervent wish—May the language and the polite literature of the Swedish nation, under the auspices which it now enjoys, attain their summit by a progress as rapid as did our military glory in the reign of GUSTAVUS-ADOLPHUS! This is no presumptuous wish, if we recollect the advances which the Swedish language has already made, and if we advert to the present state of literature among us. We have instances, in which our language has expressed, with an energy worthy of Greece and Rome, and perhaps surpassing every modern language, the most bold, sublime, and generous sentiments of liberty. We have heard it, by the irresistible power of eloquence, dissipate prejudices, convey truths, suppress one sensation, excite another, subdue inveterate antipathies, recal unanimity; warm, excite, transport; and, by its varied and yet united effects, infuse into the mind acquiescence and conviction. We possess compositions of the utmost excellence in point of lucid order, force, depth of thought, chastity of expression, neatness, harmony, elegance, and variety of style. Some are distinguished by that vigour, and that precision of genius, in which the ancients excelled, and which the moderns have found so difficult to attain. It is worthy of notice, that the authors who have charmed the public most, are those who have had the least occasion to adopt foreign expressions. Our poetry, we can assert without partiality, is in a higher degree of perfection than the poetry of most other nations at the period when they began to cultivate their language. The epic poem, the ode, the drama, evince that the Swedish language is sublime, masculine, pathetic, flexible, and sonorous; while our philosophic poems prove it energetic, ingenious, clear, and expressive. In *Atis* and *Camilla* (it is allowable to cite this masterly performance,

formance, fince its author is no more), the fire, the impetuofity of love, the language of fentiment, the riches of nature, and the power of beauty, are felt and acknowledged. In other poetic compofitions, tendernefs, vivacity, fportivenefs, and warmth, have united with terms the moſt expreffive of delicate love, of refinement, of raillery, and of mirth. Our fatire is not deftitute of point, our tales are not wanting in elegance, nor our fables deficient in a noble fimplicity of ftyle. If fome branches of Swedifh literature remain ftill uncultivated, if feveral have not attained to maturity, we have every reafon to hope that the period of their perfection will foon arrive; fince the experience of hiftory informs us, that genius never fails to flourifh when foftered by the dew of royal munificence.

It is not, however, as a collective body, that this academy can expect to enrich our language with thofe mafterpieces which are ftill wanting to our literature : fuch works can only be produced by the fire and force of a fingle genius. But if, among the members of this learned fociety, fome appear, who have received from the hand of nature fuperior abilities, who, from a knowledge of men and an acquaintance with books, have acquired a folid tafte, and have been encouraged by public approbation—by what new degree of force will they be animated, when incited in the career of glory by him to whofe hands the nation has committed the tafk of rewarding merit? Should even the glory of arriving at the fublimeft heights of Parnaffus be referved to no perfon of our number, yet we cannot deceive ourfelves when we prefume, that the recompenfes we diftribute may one day excite a genius, who fhall reach the point

which

which we have as yet been unable to attain; that the situation which we now occupy, and the advantages which are attached to it, may operate on that genius as powerful motives to double his activity, to repel the insults of ignorant contempt, to vanquish despair, and to prevent his yielding to disgust at the sight of that injustice which so frequently discourages the rising talents of men of merit. Some, indeed, from the impulse of their irresistible mental powers, and actuated by a consciousness of their own abilities, have dared and surmounted every obstacle. But how much greater is the number of those, whose talents have been crushed under the pressure of distress, or whose genius has been buried in oblivion! What class of men require more encouragement than men of letters? What is the end and object of their toils? It is not gain, except as far as an unequal distribution of riches induces the poor to consider as wealth that which merely suffices to supply the exigencies of life. Still less is it their object to arrive at court promotion, which to them must be unsolicited. Is it then fame? Undoubtedly. But from whom do they expect it? from their contemporaries, or from posterity? If they aspire at the enjoyment of reputation during their life-time, at what an exorbitant rate must it be obtained? How many vexations and disappointments are they condemned to undergo? They must oppose a spirit of pride, which beholds every surrounding object with infinite contempt; they must encounter ignorance, which affects to judge of what it does not understand; they must combat with prejudice and narrowness of mind, whose characteristic is selfishness; they must be vulnerable to envy, which delights in calumniating merit, and to levity, which sacrifices every thing to the

temptation

temptation of a jest. The idle of every kind, who wish to augment their own number, deny the utility of literature; and the effusions of genius are exposed to the decisions of that class of men, who, moving in a more exalted sphere, affect to regulate the opinions of others, but are themselves too enervated to feel, too much distracted to reflect before they pronounce sentence, too little alive to the pleasure of existence to be capable of amusement, or, if roused for a moment from their lethargy, soon revert to their wonted indifference, and repeat their usual decision, equally short and equally judicious—*What tedious stuff!*

I DIVERT with pleasure your attention from a picture which happily will not in future find an archetype among us. The opening prospect of Swedish literature is highly agreeable; and our functions would be equally so, were they confined to the obligations of contributing, according to our abilities, to the progress of literature, to the encouragement of rising genius, and to the task of exploring and honouring those who have arrived at a maturity of merit. But we have another field to cultivate— a field, the thorns and briars of which would soon deter the courage of a single genius — a field which the public cannot cultivate, because they could never agree on the manner in which it ought to be improved, and which a single man could never clear, because he would be perpetually exposed to the mistakes of prejudice and self-love. You cannot but perceive, gentlemen, that I speak of that grammar, which the academy is directed to compose. The difficulties attached to this labour need not be recapitulated to you, to whom they are well known; nor to the enlightened

lightened public that furround us, who are too equitable not to fee that much time will be required before a work of fo much difficulty can be carried to perfection. But, what affords to me, who am one day to confign to the annals of hiftory the labours of this fociety, the greateft pleafure is the conviction I entertain of your zeal for the public good, your averfion to all ufurped authority, your defign to eftablifh your decifions on the bafis of the moft correct criticifm, and to commit their truth or fallacy to the touchftone of argument and reafon.

If on a future day we fhould be happy enough to eftablifh, on a folid bafis, the orthography of our language, the certain principles and rules of compofition, and to procure to the Swedes what they are ftill in want of, a compleat dictionary—fhall we then have acquitted ourfelves of all that the public have a right to expect from the Swedifh academy? No, gentlemen, the honour which our fociety has of being diftinguifhed by the national name, impofes upon us duties of a permanent nature. We are bound to the utmoft of our power to maintain the genuine character of the language, which, like the nation, is mafculine, bold, elevated, and ferious. We are bound to exhibit in our works an example of refpect for religion, for the government, for the nation, and for morality; to prevent, as far as depends upon our activity and influence, youthful genius from being deluded by the *ignis fatuus* of fugitive fame, and facrificing to the ambition of wit, the intereft of religion, the fentiments of decency, and the duties of a citizen.

AN ORATION BY M. DE ROSENSTEIN.

CONVINCED of your earnest desire to devote yourselves to your several duties, I have here taken the liberty of sketching them to your view. One still remains, of all, perhaps, the most difficult; I mean the preservation of taste. What is taste? Where are the judges of taste? Is it the public? The public are liable to be seduced. Were it not so, taste would be privileged from corruption. Is it the race of authors? They are subject to errors and mistakes; and their blemishes serve frequently to mislead others. Shall it be a society? Who has invested them with a right, which no sovereign can assume? Is it an individual? Who has conferred this honour upon him? The foundations of taste are, however, not the less certain; and her temple rests upon two immoveable pillars—Feeling, which invents without the aid of reflection, and Reason, which subjects every thing to her enquiry. But it will be alledged, that feeling and reason are not unfrequently at variance with each other. I will, however, venture to assert, that they are never so much in opposition as not to be easily reconciled, except it be amongst those, whose exalted opinion of their own abilities prompts them to prefer their own individual taste to the sense of the public, and their own sentiments to the sentiments of others. Amongst different nations, we may indeed discover a difference of taste; but all enlightened countries agree in the essential principles. An individual, who should take his own caprice for a guide, may be disgusted with VIRGIL; another may condemn OVID as too frivolous, and blame BOILEAU for his frigidity; a third may condemn QUINAULT, because he is effeminate: but the majority of genuine connoisseurs will ever read with pleasure and admiration the *Æneid*, the *Metamorphoses*, the works of Boileau, and the *Operas* of Quinault. It must indeed be allowed, that writers of a bad taste have frequently found readers, and even admirers: but posterity has never failed to condemn their works to eternal oblivion; and their names are known only by the victorious pleasantries of contemporary critics.

Permit me, gentlemen, to make one observation in this place, which time will not, however, permit me to develope at full length. The history of letters evinces, that the false taste which has preceded the brilliant ages of literature, has ever been eradicated by the true; but that after a purity of taste had triumphed for some time, a bad taste, different from the first, began to insinuate itself, increased by little and little, and at last obtained an evil ascendancy.

The literature of this country has not yet arrived at that point, from which, according to the ordinary fate of human labour, a fall is to be feared. But are we therefore exempt from danger? It must not be dissembled, that the cultivation of the *Belles Lettres* amongst us commenced at a period later than with other nations, who, on account of priority, have acquired in some degree the right of serving us as models. But if amongst some of these nations the corruption of taste be already commenced; if a people, whose compositions have been praised for purity of taste, exquisite elegance, and simple grace, begin already to degenerate into a style affected, turgid, and disgraced with quaint conceit and far-fetched ornaments; if a nation, distinguished by vigorous thoughts and

energetic

energetic expreſſions, exhibits no longer its ancient, maſculine, and nervous taſte, and has at the ſame time the mortification of ſeeing that in ſeveral countries abroad writers pretend to reſemble their celebrated authors, by imitating their defects and their ſingularities; if amongſt another nation, who have propoſed nature and the feelings of the heart as the principal objects of their literature, authors ſhould be found, who are accuſed, not unjuſtly, of having overcharged their images and expreſſions; if all theſe defects really exiſt amongſt thoſe nations, ought it not to be our firſt care to preſerve ourſelves from the contagion of their example, and ſhould we not be careful to examine whether any of thoſe blemiſhes begin already to infect our literature?

I AM not preſumptuous enough to decide the queſtion; but I will only aſk, Have we always been careful to diſtinguiſh our own feelings from the ſentiments which we may expect to excite in others; the ſenſe which we may attach internally to our expreſſions, from the ſenſe in which the ſame expreſſions will moſt probably ſtrike our readers; and our own ſelf-complacency, from the approbation of the public? Have we never miſtaken an empty prodigality of exclamation for the language of paſſion, confuſion for genius, obſcurity for depth, and bombaſt for ſublimity? Have we always well examined what additions the prevailing thought and principal ſentiment will bear, without being weakened and concealed by the acceſſory expreſſions, which ſhould only ſerve to throw a greater light upon the firſt, and to give more life to the latter?

AN ORATION BY M. DE ROSENSTEIN.

WHO shall reply to these questions? If we addrefs ourselves to literary men, we shall find them divided in opinion: but if, in order to decide this question, we call to our affistance an art, which has the moft exact refemblance to the *Belles Lettres*, at leaft to poetry, the painter will inform us, that he is permitted to conceal on the canvas a part of the thought, but that it is never allowable to miflead the fpectator by glaring colours and falfe light. If we confult nature, fhe will inftruct us that the paffions have a tone which excites an emotion proportioned to their energy; but that this tone becomes difgufting and unpleafant, if raifed too high. Nature alfo tells us, that the Alps excite admiration, not when clouds conceal them from our view, but when the excurfive eye meets with no obftacle but the towering immenfity of the mountain. As for us, there is another mode of deciding the queftion: it is to regard with diffidence our own opinion, and to turn our eyes to thofe immortal works, which, confecrated by the unanimous approbation of fucceffive ages, of various nations and periods differing in character, have acquired a right to be regarded as the models of genius and tafte.

OBSERVATIONS

ON

TASTE AND POLITE LITERATURE,

DELIVERED BEFORE A GENERAL ASSEMBLY OF THE SWEDISH ACADEMY,

DECEMBER 20, 1787,

BY

M. DE ROSENSTEIN,

COUNSELLOR TO THE GRAND COUNCIL OF THE ROYAL CHANCERY, &c. &c.

A SUMMARY OF THE AUTHOR'S PLAN.

A View of the Fluctuation of Opinion respecting the Belles Lettres, *of which, however, the Author contends, the Principles are as certain as those of the Generality of Sciences.—Objections to the Tendency of* Polite Literature *considered.—Different Theories concerning them.—A middle Plan proposed.—The Advantage which may be derived from a theoretical Knowledge of elegant Learning.—An Answer to some Objections against the Effects of Literature on Society.*

OBSERVATIONS

ON

TASTE AND POLITE LITERATURE,

BY

M. DE ROSENSTEIN.

IF the opinions of mankind are unstable, wavering, and contradictory; if two persons, whose manner of thinking perfectly coincides, are as difficult to be found, as two whose features have a perfect resemblance, there seems at first view to be no subject, to which this observation is more apposite, than to Taste and the *Belles Lettres*. There are sciences, which, founded on the clearest evidence of our senses, are certain not only in their principles, but in their consequences. There are others, in which experience has rendered at least some truths indisputable. History, which

rests

rests on the veracity of testimony, becomes certain, when this veracity cannot be called in question. The abstract sciences, it is true, which pretend to elevate our meditations beyond the compass of the senses, have not seldom partaken of that distraction which too commonly infests the minds of those who cultivate them. By fixing the memory of words, and by marking the boundary where enquiry should stop and ignorance be acknowledged, Philosophy however has been able to evince, that the various opinions which prevail among mankind, arise from terms rather than from things. If certainty has not hence been attained, a limit at least has been placed to conjecture, subtilty, and confusion. Placed in a rank too elevated to be subjected to the investigation of an ignorant and unreflecting multitude, the sciences are in general not exposed to their rash and injudicious decisions. The success of these superior branches of study has depended upon enlightened minds, whose contests, though disgraceful to literature, yet, as they are conducted by a systematic chain of reasoning, and rest on fixed principles, may possibly admit of being reconciled.

Of all these advantages Polite Literature appears on the first view to be destitute. Though calculated to excite the best feelings of the human heart, the imagination is subject not only to the criticism of mankind, but to what is still more vague and changeable, their humours. By these standards decisions are given. Sensibility ought to be a sure guide: yet how variable are the feelings of men! On different persons how different their effects! How many schemes have been put in practice to stifle their voice, and to mislead their dictates? Do they not themselves

themselves frequently require the direction of reason and experience? How much, consequently, do the judgments of mankind differ respecting works of taste? One man condemns what another praises: what some deem worthy of fame, others consign to oblivion. The Individual frequently differs from himself: youth is enchanted by that, which loses part of its influence in maturer years, and in old age becomes unpleasant. A whole nation adores an author who is despised by another: though deified in England, SHAKESPEARE is ridiculed on the other side of the Channel. To the taste of Europeans, authors are disgustful who excite the veneration of Oriental nations. A work, which in one century has obtained the highest encomiums, in the next is scarcely known, or if known, it is only to be contemned.

THE changes also which taste has undergone, seem to afford another argument against the certainty of its principles. How numerous are the judges who pretend to decide on subjects of taste? With respect to mathematical works, the value is determined only by mathematicians. Though in the practice of their art, physicians are compelled to suffer an unworthy competition, yet their writings are not criticised, except by those who possess some knowledge of medicine. The philosopher is either not read, or read only by philosophers: should uninstructed readers attempt to peruse such an author, they are generally polite enough to conclude, that his work, though above their comprehension, may possibly possess truth and utility.

FAR from experiencing the same degree of candour are the votaries of elegant learning; for who does not esteem himself sufficiently qualified to judge of what is beautiful, sublime, and pathetic? The *Belles Lettres* are destined to amuse: whoever, therefore, is in search of amusement, will condemn a work which deceives his expectations. It would be in vain to plead the utility of such a performance; a quality which even the most finished works of taste are hardly allowed to possess. With the utmost freedom every one praises and condemns: hence BOILEAU was prompted to say, and of the votaries of elegant learning he said truly, that every author is the slave of the purchaser of his work.

IN opposition, however, to this true picture of the destiny of the *Belles Lettres*, another equally true may however be exhibited; a picture which appears to destroy the arguments already advanced.

BEHOLD the fame of HOMER, VIRGIL, and HORACE—of DEMOSTHENES and CICERO—of THUCYDIDES, LIVY, and TACITUS, resting on the foundation of ages, unshaken by any hostile attacks, victorious even over ridicule, that most formidable of all weapons which can be directed against genius.

FREQUENT those theatres where mankind meet to be delighted, where the emotion of one insensibly kindles sympathy in the breast of another, where praise frequently precedes judgment. Find an audience, if there exist such a one, which has nature for its guide, whose object is pleasure,

whose

whose aversion is dulness; who think it no disparagement to follow the dictates of the heart, nor affect by criticism a studied parade of genius.

OBSERVE this assembly dissolved in tears at the fate of *Britannicus*, the grief of *Andromache*, the danger which threatens *Iphigenia*: behold them appalled with terror at the alarming situation of *Merope*: see them glowing with patriotic zeal and the love of liberty, while they listen to the generous sentiments of *Emilia* and the elder *Horatius*: observe them petrified with horror on beholding the dreadful cup in which *Atreus* presents to *Thyestes* the blood of his unhappy son.

REMARK also the triumphs of the Comic Muse, and observe the same assembly making the vaulted roofs resound with shouts and acclamations at the exhibition of *Harpagon*, or the Miser, *Jourdain*, *Diaforius*, and *The Learned Ladies*: attend to the universal bursts of applause, when, after exposing the folly of an author's reciting his compositions in public, *Vadius* draws from his pocket his own verses: observe a similar effect, when *Francaleu* mistakes for a mere theatrical representation a real interview between a father and son. Who is so insensible as to be a spectator of the character of *Ariste*, the Hypocrite, or the Boaster, without at once imagining himself on the great theatre of the world?

TRUTH is the life of all, and thence the beautiful and sublime derive their force; and, whether pleased in the closet, or ravished in the playhouse, by the masterpieces of CORNEILLE, RACINE, VOLTAIRE, MOLIERE,

Moliere, or Piron, which of you can refuse to these authors a perfect knowledge of the human heart, a brilliancy of genius, beauty of style, and a taste purified and correct?

Of the power of eloquence among the ancients we are not ignorant. We remember Demosthenes by his oratory arming a pusillanimous and enervated people, extorting admiration from a rival while he drove him into exile: Cicero governing a turbulent and wavering multitude, and melting to compassion and forgiveness the obdurate purpose of Cæsar himself. At so considerable a distance of time, under circumstances so different, the speeches of these immortal orators still produce impressions which preserve their fame unrivalled in the estimation of those whose imaginations can transport them to the assemblies of Greece and Rome. Can any one fancy himself living before the battle of Cheronæa, and peruse the Oration of Demosthenes against Philip, without forming an ardent wish to behold Athens declare war against the Macedonian Conqueror? Who, in reading Tully, is not the partizan of Marcellus?

With less frequent and less considerable opportunities for exertion, modern eloquence often displays striking proofs of its efficacy. So deeply affected were the auditors of Bossuet at his Discourse on the Death of the Duchess of Orleans, that after pronouncing the words, "the Princess is no more," he was obliged to pause for some time, to allow to the tears and sighs of the assembly an undisturbed utterance. The

melancholy

melancholy viciſſitudes of worldly bliſs, pomp, and glory, are exhibited in ſuch a pathetic view in this maſterly night-piece, that it cannot be contemplated without exciting congenial emotions: nor can the eulogy, conſecrated by the ſame ſublime genius to the memory of the great CONDE, be peruſed without venerating the character of the hero and the exalted genius of the orator, without experiencing feelings equally ſtrong, though oppoſite, in contemplating the dignity and the inſignificance of man.

AMONG free nations, in the aſſemblies of the people or of their repreſentatives, eloquence frequently produces effects not inferior to thoſe which were exhibited in ancient times. At the reconciliation of jarring opinions, unanimous applauſe has often confeſſed a power operating upon mankind more ſtrongly than prepoſſeſſions, more effectually than ſelf-intereſt. It is unneceſſary to recur to foreign countries, to exemplify an aſſertion atteſted by our own annals and our own experience.

IN reading the pathetic ſpeech of the firſt GUSTAVUS to the ſtates of the kingdom, do we not burſt into tears as warm, and breathe forth bleſſings as fervent, as thoſe excited by that great monarch, when for the laſt time he addreſſed the Swediſh people. Eloquence, the ſceptre of GUSTAVUS-ADOLPHUS, ſupported the throne of CHARLES-GUSTAVUS. By eloquence, STENBOCK, a name worthy to rank with that of kings, inſpired courage into huſbandmen, converted them into warriors, and obtained relief to the kingdom from thoſe very hands which diſcontent and avarice ſeemed determined to cloſe.

ON our own experience I am not permitted to dwell, convinced that the feelings of this aſſembly render every illuſtration unneceſſary *.

OF the univerſal energy of literature many other proofs might be adduced. Authors might be mentioned, who are peruſed with freſh delight by every nation. From moſt of the branches of elegant learning examples and illuſtrations might be adduced, were I not confined to the moſt

* It has been obſerved, in a miſcellany entitled *Melanges de Litterature Suédoiſe*, publiſhed at Paris in 1788, that the firſt Swediſh poets have ever been found among the firſt order of the State; and we may alſo remark, that ſince the acceſſion of the houſe of VASA, eloquence has been inſeparable from the name of GUSTAVUS.

It was eloquence, which, raiſing GUSTAVUS-ERICSON from the rank of a private gentleman, placed him on the throne; it was the eloquence of VASA which reſcued Sweden from foreign tyranny, and which, ſince that propitious period, has not ceaſed to be the tutelary genius of that kingdom. Of this GUSTAVUS III. has afforded more than one ſtriking proof, eſpecially when at the Revolution, which he effected in 1772, he declared with energy, that he aſpired only to be the firſt citizen of a free nation:—GUSTAVUS, for whom the ſecret and inſidious attempts of an ambitious neighbouring Court, by endeavouring to revive the hydra which he defeated in 1772, have ſerved only to prepare materials for new triumphs.

His illuſtrious brother, CHARLES, Duke of Sudermannia, crowned with the youthful glory of a victory obtained over the valour of the veteran GREIGH, returned from the boiſterous fields of martial renown, to reſtore tranquillity to a no leſs ſtormy ocean at home. After having given his fellow-citizens proofs of valour, he gave them alſo an example of loyalty. By a ſpeech diſtinguiſhed for its nervous ſimplicity, he infuſed into the boſom of his audience the patriotic flame that burns in his own. He exemplified QUINTILIAN's obſervation, that the heart is the only ſource of true eloquence †.

† *Pectus eſt quod diſertus facit.*

Remark of the Tranſlator.

remarkable

remarkable. Thofe impreffions only I have pointed out, which, being fleet and volatile, ftand in need of a certain principle, to become general and lafting. I have omitted obfervations refpecting general tafte, as they would carry us into refearches of a nature too abftrufe for the prefent occafion.

But how fhall we account for the oppofite forms in which this fubject prefents itfelf? In one view fo much certainty, fo much doubt in the other. By what means fhall we reconcile the confonant fentiments of nations with the diverfity of their tafte; the unaltered admiration with the varied judgments of ages; the uniform effects recorded, with the opinions maintained in converfation refpecting the invincible authority of fafhion? What fhall we fay to the carpings of critics, to the condemnation of the unfeeling, to the remarks of the ignorant, to the exaggeration of enthufiafts, and to the cold precifion of philofophers?

Perhaps, concluding at firft fight that thefe contrarieties are irreconcileable, we fhall regard tafte and literature either with that carelefs indifference, that wavering uncertainty fo eafily adopted by the unthinking, or by that fyftematic fcepticifm which philofophers find it fo difficult to avoid. Moft of the difputes upon this fubject, I am however willing to hope, might be prevented, and fome degree of certainty obtained, if, by inveftigating the caufes of variance, thofe which conftantly operate were diftinguifhed from thofe derived from ignorance, prejudice, and folly; if, by fixing the meaning of words and ideas, we could trace opinions to their fource.

A sense

A SENSE of the utility of such a design has prompted me to attempt a subject, which, although accurately investigated by foreign writers, seems not, in our own country, to have met with the attention it deserves. Since, as secretary to the academy, I am, on solemn occasions, permitted to deliver my sentiments before so respectable an assembly, that privilege, I presume, cannot be used more agreeably to my fellow academicians, than when, under the guidance of those models, which they have thought worthy of consulting, I endeavour to discriminate the grand principles of taste, and to determine the degree of certainty of which they are susceptible.

IN executing this design, I discharge at the same time the most delightful of duties, by expressing the gratitude of the academy to its august founder and generous protector, as this cannot be more forcibly exhibited than by procuring esteem for pursuits which he vouchsafes to encourage. This esteem must be supported by certainty and conviction. Though perpetually exposed to deceit and error, man, thirsting after truth, cannot rest from painful research till he arrives at some undoubted conclusion. The most enchanting pleasures vanish, when we begin to disbelieve their principles. On the least suspicion of fallacy, our adoration is converted into contempt. Behold that idol, to whom with profound veneration the prostrate million look up: destroy the persuasion of its divinity, and suddenly the mighty god will change to a shapeless block of marble, and not a single worshipper will approach his desolated shrine.

In the course of my experience, I have met with many who affect to despise the enthusiasm of literature. The thoughtless and insensible ridicule pleasures which they cannot relish; by sneer and ridicule they endeavour to console themselves for praises which provoke their envy, and thus endeavour to stifle that secret and uneasy feeling which is excited by a consciousness of their own imbecility. Men of sense often deny their applause to works of genius, because destitute of that truth and certainty, which they think alone entitled to their esteem. Philosophers I have seen guilty of the same injustice: those philosophers I mean, who, assuming, without really deserving that honourable title, mistake for a knowledge of human nature a cavilling disposition; who, incapable of deriving from philosophy the advantages it is able to produce, know neither how to praise nor to condemn with impartiality, ignorant as they are, that there are few objects which do not in some degree merit the attention of a sage. Politicians also have thought it their duty to condemn elegant learning as useless and injurious to society. More than one PLATO, more than one JEAN JACQUES ROUSSEAU, have wished to banish literature from their republic; though few have had the address to turn against the object of their proscriptions those burnished arms of rhetoric, which those celebrated writers received from the arsenal of those very arts which they affect to despise.

It would be a trespass upon your time to bestow on ignorance arguments intelligible only to candid minds. But since I venture to defend the study of literature, it will be proper to answer some objections offered against

against its nature and tendency. This will be the more requisite, as it will afford me an opportunity of entering more minutely into the spirit of so interesting a science.

By mentioning science, a word which many will think improperly applied, I am apprehensive of exposing this subject to one of the most formidable objections, its want of a solid foundation. Knowing no certain principles, it is alledged, by which to estimate the merit of a single work of taste, how much less shall we be able to establish a general theory for the fine arts! Though with a view to effect this, numberless works have been written; though in all ages, mankind, speaking of a general taste, have endeavoured to point out its rules; though a modern nation has given to this science a new appellation *: yet many, I doubt not, regarding such attempts as frivolous, deny the reality of a general taste, consider rules rather as the shackles than as the guides of genius, and ridicule that credulity which eagerly grasps at a shadow. Let it however be our endeavour to pass a more equitable sentence.

Previously to define Taste and Polite Literature would be inconsistent with our intentions. If the essay which I meditate should be fortunate enough to find readers, at least they shall not accuse me of obtruding my own opinions. Aspiring to nothing further than to direct the reader to exercise his sensibility and judgment, I shall only premise, that,

* The Theory of *Belles Lettres* and the Fine Arts is called in Germany *Æsthotic*, i. e. applying to the feelings.

independent of other qualities, Polite Literature eminently possesses the power of pleasing, and that Taste is the faculty which enables us to judge of that power.

Those who have written concerning Polite Literature and Taste in general, have pursued two very different paths.

From works of genius, possessed of an established reputation, some authors have deduced rules for composition; supposing that admiration will always attend upon what has acquired applause, and regarding decisions already pronounced, as documents for the formation of our sentiments, by an attention to which we may anticipate the opinions of succeeding ages. Without seeming to have entirely forgotten that an unerring judgment can only be derived from an intuitive knowledge of nature, they have in general trusted too implicitly to the authority of human opinion. It is, however, by a close attention to nature alone, that a person can learn to animate his own writings, or to read with instruction the works of others.

Remounting to this source of genuine science, others indeed, by an appeal to nature, have fixed upon this as the only criterion by which to decide upon the talents of authors, and the taste of readers.

Of these two modes of judging, the former has necessarily preceded the latter, which is doubtless the most reasonable. Both, however, are liable to extremes.

By representing compositions of acknowledged merit as infallible models for imitation, exclusive rules have been constituted, which, warping the powers of the mind, instead of giving them freer scope, clip the soaring pinions of fancy, stifle all vigour of sentiment, and smother the flame of genius. Hence arise critics, who, equally useless to the world, and injurious to literature, check the rising talents of youth, imbitter the pleasures of maturer years, and seem only calculated to deprive readers of that satisfaction they would otherwise feel, and authors of that fame which too commonly is their only recompense.

Those, on the contrary, whose endeavours have been always directed to discover in the human mind the principles of taste, have written in a manner often totally destitute of that taste which they pretend to define, characterized by didactic dulness. Such works have prompted youthful genius to turn disdainfully aside from instruction, which could neither elevate the fancy, nor interest the heart.

To some favourite models the one party sacrifices experience, the other to systems; the one despises groundless and exceptionable rules, the other rejects principles and consequences because inapplicable.

Erroneous extremes thus exhibited, will, doubtless, to reflecting minds, suggest an intermediate mode of judging, partaking of the advantages of both, and free from the inconveniences of either. At once philosophical and elegant, this method may, with classic models, unite investigation,

investigation, reasoning with feeling, a veneration for works of extraordinary merit with a still greater veneration for truth, rules with those exceptions to which every rule is subject, and laws with the freedom of genius, the ardour of sensibility, and the soarings of imagination.

But of a science thus constituted what will be the nature? How shall its principles be defined? Will they admit of a scientific stability?

This science, I reply, will resemble every other species of human knowledge, in so far as it is the united result of industry and observation; a combination of experiments, with few reflections, few conclusions, and still fewer rules and principles. By giving to Polite Literature such a philosophical theory, a successful writer may deserve the appellation of a philosopher of taste. Far from such a man be that systematic superciliousness, which, benumbing the faculties of the mind by synthetic chains, oppresses sensibility with the yoke of argument. Though reasoning analytically, may he never be unmindful of the source of all knowledge; that volume, which, well studied, would, by rendering most other books unnecessary, be more destructive to many learned libraries than the desolating fire of merciless barbarians.

That great volume is experience, and of this experience we ourselves are the principal subjects. All nature operates upon our senses, whether beautiful or tremendous, magestic or mild, gay or awful. Ideas are created in the human mind by the impressions of external objects; these

ideas,

ideas, arranged into various groups, independently of the general name of science, acquire a particular appellation, according to their respective combinations. Within our own breasts exist riot and rage, boisterous passions, which, breaking forth under various forms, give birth to so many virtues and vices, to so many noble and mean actions, and which generate or dissolve human societies; passions which ought to animate the ample page of history, and which the law should restrain by punishment, or by an adequate reward direct to proper objects; passions which policy should use and govern, morality check and dignify; which poets and orators should delight to paint, to awaken, or to sooth. Within our own minds reside those tender emotions, those delicate feelings, which afford the richest colours for the pencil of genius.

If then nature, not with regard to its inanimate qualities, but to its power of operating on the human mind; if the feelings, emotions, and passions, be the originals which the votary of taste should perpetually keep in view; if fine writing be nothing else than a knowledge of the art of pleasing, a power of feeling and of judging, whence, except from the perceptions and faculties of the human soul, shall we trace the theory of taste and composition?

The first and surest method of acquiring this knowledge is, to look with a scrutinizing eye into our own breast. Here we find predominant inclinations, tumultuous passions, and gentle emotions; we observe hidden sparks of genius, which, though seldom blown into a flame, supply an inexhauftible fund of valuable materials to thofe minds which poffefs the talent of employing them to the beft advantage.

To judge by our own experience of the attainments of others, and to meafure their difpofitions by our own, is frequently fallacious and unjuft. With the ftudy, therefore, of ourfelves, fhould be joined the lefs certain, but more eafily acquired reflections, which an attention to the conduct and deportment of others enables us to form; for, perceiving in others feelings that are wanting in ourfelves, we learn to reduce to their real value our own fentiments, to try them by a ftandard authorized by fociety, to elevate or fink them to a degree capable of being communicated to the others. Hence we are taught how to command conviction, and to fhake the foul.

From the inftruction which private fociety affords, we advance to a wider field of information, opened by the world and hiftory. The contemplation of different nations and different ages enlarges our conceptions. Enabled to extend our influence beyond furrounding objects, we acquire the means of earning the veneration of mankind in future times.

Upon this immenfe ftock of knowledge the man of letters may graft the theory of an art, which fenfibility and genius qualify him to exercife, but which fhould always be directed by an enlightened tafte. On the fame bafis, though on a different plan, the lawgiver, ftatefman, and
moralift,

moralift, build their fyftems. Hence, we prefume to fay, that the knowledge of Polite Literature and Tafte may acquire a degree of certainty almoft equal to that which belongs to morality, politics, and legiflation, or to any fcience relative to human nature.

From this intimation, it may be expected that I ought more precifely to determine the nature and limits of the prefent defign.

These expectations can be anfwered only in a hafty and imperfect manner, in the introduction to a treatife, which was merely intended to contain general obfervations upon certain parts of this fcience; as I am refolved to deduce conclufions from genuine principles alone.

In what fhould the theory of Polite Literature confift, but in its being a picture of the impreffions which nature makes upon our fenfes; our feelings, emotions, paffions; and of their power of exciting approbation or difguft, pleafure or pain? It is the art of difcriminating the various taftes of different nations, ages, ranks, and perfons; an enquiry into the means of affecting the mind with delight or admiration. The groundwork of the whole is the knowledge of mankind, derived from a comprehenfive experience. By affording matter for inveftigation, elegant compofitions, and the hiftory of polite learning, will exercife the judgment, and give an idea of particular and general tafte. Not intended as legiflators, great authors will ferve only as models and guides.

If

If any one, however, imagines that such a theory will terminate all differences of opinion; if he thinks laws can be established, by which authors may infallibly be taught to please universally, and to escape the shafts of criticism, neither this subject nor my plan has been sufficiently understood.

Doubts and disputes will ever exist respecting the liberty of human opinion. A thorough knowledge of these disputes and of their origin, however valuable an acquisition, is not sufficient. Principles alone, duly ascertained, will enable us to form equitable judgments, to approve at least what we do not highly admire, and to give every author his due tribute of commendation. Diffidence in maintaining our own sentiments, and respect for those of others, will be the result of this theory. Anticipating the effect of their works, authors may foresee when they will be generally read, or when an attention to them will be confined to a certain class of mankind. Consoled by the applause of some for the disregard of others, they will not pant for an unattainable degree of fame, but direct their views to a degree of perfection which may ensure to them the esteem of an enlightened posterity.

Though subject to several defects, this theory ought not on that account to be despised, since all other sciences are in some measure liable to the same objection. Morality will serve us for an example. In this important science is there nothing controvertible? It ought to be founded on fixed principles: but these are only determined by reason and feeling, which frequently contend for victory. Are these principles powerful enough to compel nations, or even individuals, to think and act alike ? Can they bind opposite characters by the ties of affection and friendship ? Will morality ever be able to appease the perpetual contest between honour and duty ; between private and public obligations ; between imperious opinions and restricting laws ; between humanity pleading for pardon, and social order demanding vindictive punishment; between that justice which examines the motives of an action, and that which considers its legality and its consequences ? Can moral science create estimable qualities without their attendant failings ? Has it ever formed a completely virtuous character ? or has it only been able, by shewing the origin of contrarieties, to render enlightened persons equitable in their judgments and in their conduct ; some few, as perfect, or rather as little imperfect, as human nature will admit ? Yet, who will say that morality should be treated with distrust or neglect ?

But allowing the possibility of a theory of Polite Literature, to what purpose, it may be asked, will it serve ?

This question may be expected from those, who have observed many persons, possessed of a theoretic knowledge of composition, who yet were incapable of a single flight of genius, and destitute of taste ; while others, though unaided by learning, by the sole guidance of nature, decide with accuracy, and even compose with elegance.

HAVING

Having already in part anfwered this objection, as I wifh not to impofe my opinions as authorities, the reft of my reply I will referve, till my reafoning fhall coincide with the conclufions of the reader. A few obfervations, however, may not be improper; efpecially as they will be fupported by examples from arts, of which mankind judge lefs vaguely than of the *Belles Lettres*.

In obferving that nature opens an inexhauftible ftore for the votaries of Tafte, I own that genius, by its warmth and brilliancy, and fenfibility, by her irrefiftible energy, can alone enable an author to infufe his own feelings into the breafts of others. That no degree of knowledge will compenfate the want of feeling, I have alfo allowed. The man to whom nature has denied genius, fhe has alfo forbidden to cultivate elegant learning with fuccefs. To the man to whom fhe has denied feeling, fhe has no lefs denied the power of judging of the feelings of others. But ought we thence to conclude that genius and fenfibility authorize contempt for the aid of experience? What, indeed, is any fcience and theory, except the refult of our own experience, affifted by that of others. Never lofing fight of life and manners, true genius ftudies mankind, nature, the world, and works of great merit, in the fame manner as an artift contemplates animate and inanimate creation, and the works of thofe mafters who have moft fuccefsfully imitated both. Without that imagination, that happy enthufiafm, which ftamps on works of fancy a lafting character, the painter and ftatuary would never acquire fame: yet, how unfuccefsful would be their efforts, without an unremitting diligence to acquire dexterity,

terity, without a steady attention to obtain a thorough knowledge of nature, without that finishing elegance suggested by the rules of art, the advice of connoisseurs, and the examples of eminent masters?

IN the qualifications of the artist are described those of the man of letters; his attention, occupied by nature, should follow theory as a guide; the example of others should supply the deficiencies of his own experience. Seldom are theory and practice distinctly ascertained. In applying what has been said of authors, to readers, or mere judges of literature, I cannot but express a wish, that these would shew a still greater share of diffidence in deciding upon works beyond their own abilities to produce.

THUS, having described the science from which I propose to deduce the principles of this subject, I have rather pointed out the eminence to which others may attain, than that to which I myself presume to aspire. In shewing the sources from which this theory must be derived, I have merely sketched its outlines. To present a full display of the different branches of elegant learning, is not my intention: but, by diffusing some general ideas of taste and composition among my young countrymen, I hope to exhibit to them a source of fresh delight, and to guard them against passing an unfair judgment upon those who rather deserve an equitable sentence, as their ambition frequently aims no farther than to the instruction and entertainment of their readers. Though in consulting those profound authors, whose insight into human nature has enabled them

them to penetrate into the deepeſt receſſes of the heart, and to unfold all its ſecret ſprings, I propoſe to extend my enquiries as far as poſſible; yet I mean to advance nothing but what is clear, and calculated to inform. The ſciences indeed require their truth to be eſtabliſhed by deep inveſtigation: every candid philoſopher will however acknowledge, that the moſt abſtract reaſoning never ſtruck out any uſeful diſcovery, which was not almoſt inſtantly adopted by the plain underſtanding of all, who were not bewildered by ſyſtems, or blinded by prejudice. The firſt duty of an author is to be intelligible, the next to be explicit. If a firſt-rate genius is thought entitled to diffuſe opinions which require explanation, a claim to ſuch a privilege muſt appear ridiculous when ſupported only by the deſire of ſingularity. Though reſolved to confine myſelf to general obſervations, yet I perceive that the extenſiveneſs and difficulty of this arduous taſk will render it impoſſible for me completely to define its nature, or to point out its preciſe limits. Both admitting of conſiderable alterations, there is no part of this attempt to be aſcertained, except the defects it will doubtleſs exhibit. Independent of a ſtill more important object, various occupations will, it is hoped, plead for the imperfections of the performance.

I CANNOT lay down the pen, without replying to one of the principal objections againſt elegant learning; an objection which has already been mentioned in alluding to thoſe who conſider Polite Literature as uſeleſs, and even pernicious to ſociety.

THEY

They give birth, it is alledged, to effeminacy, and confequently to a corruption of morals which threatens nations with political ruin.

Were I in any degree perfuaded of the truth of this affertion, I fhould be culpable in defending the ftudy of elegant learning. Could I fee with indifference my readers imbibe fuch an opinion, I fhould be regardlefs of my own reputation, of the fame of that fociety of which I have the honour to be a member, and of truth, the moft valuable of all poffeffions. It would require a feparate treatife to reply fully to every argument on which the above objection is founded. A few obfervations will be fufficient for my purpofe, if they fhould prompt others to decide a queftion, which it is my humble office only to propofe.

From the four following fources are derived thofe arguments, the grounds of which I venture to deny:—the examples recorded in hiftory; a comparifon between thofe periods in which polite learning has flourifhed, and in which it was unknown; the very nature of elegant learning; and the difpofitions and conduct of thofe who are devoted to its purfuits.

Examples deduced from hiftory I mention firft, well perfuaded that they have long and powerfully fupported the caufe of error. There is not any thing, of which mankind have been more ignorant, than of the fcience of focial life. The imperfections incident to every form of government I do not arraign. How indeed could perfection be attained,

without

without mature confideration; and who can expect mature confideration in works produced by the fortuitous courfe of events, by the tyranny of circumftances? Among the ancient ftates, Sparta alone could boaft a legiflation connected in all its parts: yet, by militating againft the ftrongeft propenfities of human nature, the Spartan laws excited a perpetual conflict, that ended in the deftruction of that country. The governments at prefent fubfifting may be aptly compared to Gothic edifices improved by the hand of tafte.

It may be obferved, that a prudent extent of territory, a comprehenfive experience, and an induftrious purfuit of happinefs, have contributed more to the public and private advantage of mankind than the moft admired laws of the ancient legiflators. There ftill, however, fubfift fo many fundamental defects and errors, fo much oppofition between different parts of the fame fyftem, that no modern form of government can be confidered as a juft model for imitation. Venice will perhaps be pointed out as an exception; a republic of which the conftitution has furvived its greatnefs, and a material change in the fentiments of the people. But what a conftitution! Equally unfhaken, Oriental defpotifm has a higher claim to antiquity.

Nevertheless, hiftory has long been confidered as affording examples for the conftruction of forms of government. Athens, Carthage, and Rome, are objects of enquiry in France, England, and Sweden. Elevating their voice, philofophers have at length ventured to afk, if

France

France be Athens, England Carthage, or Sweden Rome. Is it not, however, often afferted, that after having loft her fimplicity, frugality, and poverty, Sparta was no more; that Athens, by encouraging public fpectacles, ceafed to conquer; inftead of a MILTIADES, an ARISTIDES, a THEMISTOCLES, fhe had a MENANDER, a PLATO, a DEMOSTHENES? Charmed with the eloquence of CICERO, the poetry of VIRGIL and HORACE, the Romans fupinely neglected their country's freedom. Alarming examples thefe! alarming, indeed, for governments like thefe! But other caufes fufficiently account for the deftruction of liberty.

BY the frantic rage of conqueft, every fmall community muft fall a victim to its own weaknefs, every extenfive monarchy a prey to its own grandeur. The love of peace will not fhield the former from the attacks of an ambitious neighbour, unavoidable neceffity compels them to combat, to conquer, or to perifh. A political truth this, which will throw fome light on the ruins of ancient governments.

THE Lacedemonians, defigned by LYCURGUS to be protected by valour, from equality and poverty to derive peace and contentment, to poffefs independence by ruling only over themfelves; thefe people loft their ftrength, when, inftead of preferving a fyftem of felf-defence, they committed hoftilities upon others; engaged in war with a fuperior force, they foon ceafed to be independent; their happinefs was alike deftroyed by the confequences of victory or of adverfe fortune. Athens found it impoffible to fupport undiminifhed that vigour of mind, that heroic

valour,

valour, which, on the field of Marathon, and on the shore of Salamis, enabled a handful of men to vanquish armies numerous beyond the experience or the belief of modern times.

THAT the decline and fall of the Roman Empire, was the inevitable consequence of its extravagant ambition, who can question? But why have not those acute reasoners, who pretend to trace events to their causes, shewn, whence proceeded the destruction of those states, on whose ruin Rome raised her Collosean greatness? Was it luxury and elegant learning which destroyed the Sabines, the citizens of Veji, the Volscians, and the Latins: or did not their own weakness abandon their destiny to the chance of war? Imperious Rome herself had, more than once, nearly seen falsified her real, or pretended dreams of eternity.

WITH these events literature had not any, or at most a very slight connection. To elegant occupations Sparta paid little attention; nay, if destitute of poets and orators, Athens would have fallen like Sybaris, Capua, and unlettered Carthage. Had Rome erected her vast monarchy, without subjecting Greece; in all probability, Rome would have been little acquainted with polite learning; but, most certainly, her power, like that of Persia and Macedon, must have declined.

BUT should the influence of elegant learning be allowed to have been injurious to ancient states; at present, however, it cannot be considered in that light. This, the history and constitution of modern governments will sufficiently evince.

I   THE

The polite subjects of LEWIS XIV. were warriors not less courageous than the ruder Germans and Spaniards, whom they opposed. This monarch, the patron of polite learning, like AUGUSTUS, riveted, it is true, the fetters of slavery on the nation: yet, at the same period, amidst the flourishing growth of science and elegant learning, the English fixed on a firm basis, their admirable constitution.

How little the destiny of ancient governments ought, at present, to excite our alarm, every reflecting mind will easily perceive. Extent of territory and power are more equally distributed; envy and fear, the centinels of the strong, prove the guardians of the weak: restrained by finance, war is less calculated for conquest, than for defence; knowledge is applied to the advantage of society. Without opposing the moderate claims of the human passions, their excess only is consigned to punishment; the demands of liberty seek an equality in natural, rather than in acquired, privileges; rather private security, than political pre-eminence. An uniformity of conduct will then secure modern governments against all those calamities, which flow not from foreign and external causes. But, perhaps, I have examined, too minutely, an argument which the more intelligent adversaries of literature, will not very strenuously defend.

" To inforce our reasoning, we need not, they will alledge, have recourse
" to history, nor exhibit instances of extreme danger, to shew the necessity
" of condemning the effects of elegant learning. It is enough, if man-
" kind be more effeminate, more criminal, than in former times. If,
" from

"from our own degeneracy, we have reason to expect a progeny still more corrupt than ourselves; is our improvement in knowledge to be considered as advantageous? By giving new play to the affections, have not the pursuits of elegant learning, materially contributed to produce the evils of which we now complain?"

Prevented, as I am, by a want of leisure, not by a dread of the weight of my opponent's arguments, from replying at large to objections, on the minds of many very deeply impressed by the deluding colours of eloquence; yet a concise view of the progress of society will evince, that no comparison has been made between the advantages and evils; that, if a change of manners be a calamity, it is an unavoidable one; and that a mere effect has been preposterously mistaken for a cause.

Amidst the variety of human conditions, there is none which can boast advantages, unconnected with disadvantages. These, on the contrary, will seldom be found unalleviated, if we set aside the unnatural situations of despotism on the one hand, and of slavery and oppression on the other. The state of savages, their gradual progress in civilization, I forbear mentioning. It will not be necessary to refute those, who delight in declaiming on the felicity of barbarism, if it be considered with what difficulty savages provide for their sustenance, what ceaseless hostility they exercise against each other, and that languor clouds, and frequently shortens their monotonous lives.

TAUGHT to depend no longer for subsistence on the destruction of animals, or on the spontaneous productions of the earth, but obliged to cultivate the ground, mankind fixed on a determinate spot, though not without danger of being expelled by invaders more powerful than themselves. Such a situation the dawn of society presents to our view: but how gloomy is yet the prospect! Turning our eyes from states destroyed in their infancy; from nations, either long since buried in their ruins, or still groaning under oppression, let us, excluding circumstances merely casual, and attending to general causes, contemplate some of those people, who have passed through all the several stages from barbarism to refinement.

AFTER the means of subsistence are provided, the next desire of man, is for personal liberty. Disdaining the bonds, which prevent mankind from employing their faculties for the promotion of their happiness, liberty does not desist from her claims, till all unnecessary restraints are removed. Property once secured, produces inequality of circumstances; inequality, affording a scope to man's natural propensity to ease, engenders luxury, a subject productive of much contention among philosophers and politicians.

THIS natural progress of society, is frequently retarded or accelerated, by accidental causes. These causes exhibit a people, struggling under internal or foreign restraint, regaining lost freedom, again sinking under a superior force, until at length human nature becomes impatient of bondage, and every thing recovers its stated course. Amidst these different situations,

tions, national manners, depending on the different degrees of civilization, will undergo material changes. At firſt, rude and barbarous, then ſimple and unpoliſhed, afterwards enlightened, laſtly arriving at the higheſt pitch of politeneſs, mankind become prudent in their conduct, delicate in their converſation, and refined in their ſentiments.

FROM this ordinary progreſs, there will, however, be deviations. A people exerting all their force to defend or enlarge their territory, diſplay actions wonderful, laudable, and frequently honoured with the name of heroiſm. But this enthuſiaſm ſoon ſubſides. At other times, happy or untoward circumſtances have an extraordinary effect. To ſuch a degree of corruption the morals of men may arrive, the human mind may become ſo debaſed and effeminate, ſo willing to ſubmit to the firſt yoke which ſhall be impoſed, as to allow deſpotiſm to annihilate every idea of public virtue.

HENCE it appears, that the changes, which take place in ſociety, are of two kinds: either proceeding from accidental cauſes, or inevitably derived from the very nature of civil communities.

IF the former be productive of greater inconveniences than advantages, they may properly be arraigned, as requiring redreſs. The latter, no wiſe man will cenſure, nor attempt to place barriers againſt the uniform and irreſiſtible courſe of nature. Thoſe countries which poſſeſs the largeſt ſhare of freedom and ſecurity, the ſage will conſider as the moſt happy; as the

leaſt

least imperfect that system of laws, which imposes the smallest constraint upon the human passions. Without dwelling on defects and inconveniences, which flow from the very source of virtue, he is persuaded, that, in all ages mankind, bearing a strong resemblance to each other, are ever actuated by the same motives: ambition, envy, and self-interest. The predominance of certain virtues or vices, occasions a diversity of manners. The most estimable virtues, however, result from that state of society, in which mankind have obtained the valuable right of seeking happiness without injuring each other, and have secured this important right by established laws.

THESE observations are sufficient to disprove the answer to the censure, which has been thrown on modern times and modern manners.

IF we have clearer ideas of the rights of human nature, of the origin and aim of society; if already influencing the conduct of sovereigns, and the laws of nations, these ideas procure a more tranquil enjoyment of advantages natural or acquired: surely we have no reason to look back with an eye of envy on former times. If more humane and reasonable, more benevolent and social, our manners flow from the natural progress of civil society: then is every complaint against them as unfounded as it is insignificant. We are evidently, therefore, advanced to that degree of civilization, at which it was expedient that we should arrive; nor could its attendant inconveniences be removed, without introducing still greater evils.

How little the ancient ſtates are calculated to become examples to the modern, has already been demonſtrated.

HAVING thus endeavoured to anſwer objections, by which this ſubject has been obſcured, I may now be permited to inveſtigate the nature of polite literature, and its peculiar influence upon ſociety. This, perhaps, ought to have been my firſt object. But prejudice, oppoſed by truth, reſembles a citadel, aſſaulted by a ſuperior force: when its outworks, the principal ſtrength, are once broken down, its entire deſtruction is eaſily accompliſhed.

THE firſt idea, ſuggeſted by the Belles Lettres, demonſtrates them to be rather the conſequence than the cauſe of the manners of mankind. By civil ſociety, the mind muſt be prepared to receive their impreſſions. INACHUS, CECROPS, and DANAUS preceded AMPHION, LINUS, and ORPHEUS, who alſo, it is ſaid, ſpoke only to the ear. Before HOMER could addreſs the fancy, what further progreſs muſt not ſociety have made! Elegant learning depends on the degree of civilization, no leſs for its gradual advancement, than for its firſt riſe. Though ſince the revival of letters, the valuable remains of the ancients engage the attention of modern nations, their taſte is formed eſſentially by internal cauſes. The character of the people, for whom an author writes, muſt be ſtudied by him, if he wiſhes to ſeize the heart. The prevailing ſentiments of a nation have a conſiderable influence upon individuals. Hence the connexion, obſerved between the genius of a people and their taſte. That every material

change

change in the civilization, manners, and sentiments of mankind, has had a proportionate influence on their taste and literature, I shall endeavour to evince. Uncommon flights of genius must, however, be excepted, which soaring beyond the bounds of the present age, contribute to form the taste of posterity.

The political causes which principally influence the manners of a nation, create and perfect the Belles Lettres; these, in their turn, are not destitute of effects, for in the moral world, effects re-act upon their causes. Before the question be examined whether the influence of elegant learning be useful or injurious, the nature of this influence ought to be ascertained.

Of some few, the entire attention is devoted to polite learning: In others, by employing those vacant hours which can be spared from business or trivial pursuits, polite literature becomes a rich source of innocent pleasure, opens a large field for imagination, quickens sensibility, extends the knowledge of human nature, refines the sentiments, destroys grosser attachments, and gives birth to a more delicate choice of amusements, to more exquisite recreations, to a more enlightened intercourse. Inaccessible to all but men of science, many truths have, by the help of elegant learning, been generally diffused; and from the superiority of the objects of its enquiry, the human understanding has encreased its penetration. And can it be imagined, that such effects would be injurious? No, it is answered, not so much, on a superficial survey, as they will appear on a more accurate inspection. The pleasures of imagination are often indulged to an immo-

derate

derate degree; by refinement converfation becomes lefs fincere; the Belles Lettres, adminiftering amufements which lead to vices, and often exercifed on criminal fubjects, prove the caufes of effeminacy, and the corruptors of manners.

There is nothing, however excellent and laudable it may be, that is not fubject to inconvenience, and liable to abufe. Without entering upon a new defence of our prefent political and moral fituation, I fhall content myfelf with referring to what has already been faid refpecting the neceffity of that fituation. When we reflect, that the *Belles Lettres* cannot flourifh except amongft a people who have arrived at a certain degree of eafe and opulence, the fureft mode of afcertaining whether they are ufeful or pernicious, will be to compare two nations placed on the fame degree in the fcale of civilization, one of which cultivates the polite arts, and the other neglects them entirely. Polite literature and the fciences mutually affift each other. It is difficult to arrive at the latter, without paffing through the former: it would be madnefs to think of attaining the fciences, while the ftudy of the Belles Lettres was profcribed. It is phyfically impoffible, that the human mind fhould expatiate in the vaft field of intellectual exertion, while fo abfurd a barrier is oppofed to our progrefs. The only difference between fcience and the polite arts is this, that the firft acts more upon the underftanding, and the latter have a greater influence on manners and the conduct of life.

LET us then imagine to ourselves, as I have already observed, two nations enjoying an equal portion of security and welfare; in each of these nations will exist the same degree of sensuality and luxury, and thence in each nation will arise the same defects and the same vices.

BUT if one of these nations was destitute of elegant learning, unsusceptible of any refined pleasure, and solely addicted to sensual enjoyments, it would soon become the victim of indolence, cowardice, and effeminacy. Such has been the fate of those nations, which, without knowledge, have obtained power. Of this the Persians, Macedonians, and Turks, are sufficient examples. A similar destiny will be experienced by those people who, without attending to the cultivation of their minds, enjoy merely the conveniences of life. The European colonies are proofs of this assertion.

ON the contrary, in another nation, equally powerful and prosperous, the culture of elegant learning will produce congenial sentiments of patriotism. Independently of the diffusion of useful knowledge, polite literature excites and cherishes moral feelings, which, by restraining sensual pleasures within proper limits, excite and encourage men of talents, by the hopes of immortal fame. This is a motive, which, on the first repose of Rome from the yoke of despotism, animated the genius of TACITUS and PLINY; and which, preserving for a time the ancient grandeur of the empire, rendered less precipitate the fall of the Roman world. This argument will obtain additional force, by considering European nations, which,

which, with forms of government nearly similar, possess different degrees of knowledge.

It remains, that I should mention those faults which have been objected to the votaries of taste; faults scarcely deserving notice, when urged as serious reproaches.

The charms of poetry, it is alledged, have been prostituted in fulsome flattery upon the most unworthy monarchs. But we certainly ought not to charge poetry with its abuse. Was the sovereign, who admired and rewarded flattery, ever destitute of sycophants? To the princes who have despised or neglected literature, flatterers have not been wanting, not even to CALIGULA, who profanely wished to destroy the works of Virgil. LEWIS the XIV. has perhaps been too highly praised: but LEWIS, really great, was instigated by praise itself to noble actions. In the same age, BUTLER and DRYDEN, were allowed to languish in poverty, by CHARLES the II. while he supported ministers who encouraged his effeminate indolence, and courtiers who entertained his voluptuous levity. Let us view mankind as they are. Few form their own characters: those of the generality arise from circumstances. Between flattery and elegant learning there is no close connection: on the contrary, the first and most natural effect of the Belles Lettres, is to elevate the mind. But when found to be the road to preferment, adulation will alike be pursued by the indigent, the ambitious, the scholar, the courtier, and the warrior. In such a situation, men of letters deserve our utmost pity, as the monuments of

their

their genius perpetuate their dishonour. Happy the author who can safely utter truth, and who is sufficiently spirited to exercise that valuable privilege.

THE most enraptured votaries of learning, who are blessed with a fruitful and ardent imagination, are unqualified, it is affirmed, for those duties of life which require reflection: their behaviour is generally singular, and their restless mind is the sport of unruly passions.

BUT of this remark, liable to so many exceptions, what is the inference?

IT proves only, that mankind should follow the impulse and direction of nature. If they feel a strong incitement to elegant learning, why should they resist its pleasing influence? In obeying the dictates of nature, they are most likely to be useful to themselves and to society; and the fire of genius, instead of being injurious, will animate them to the pursuit of knowledge and virtue.

FAR, therefore, from being condemned, the culture of elegant learning ought to be highly encouraged. The leisure which they have devoted to the Belles Lettres, will not be regretted by those who regard them merely as an amusement; they will hence learn to arrange their thoughts, to give dignity to the passions. Capable of procuring for themselves a sublime and heart-felt satisfaction, they will despise the noisy pleasures
which

which captivate the croud. Thofe who feel themfelves impelled to devote their principal attention to polite learning, will not fail of an adequate reward.

If the Belles Lettres afford a neceffary aid to fcience; if they polifh the manners, mitigate or diminifh the pernicious effects of profperity; if they communicate pleafures frugal and profitable; if they brighten the gloom of folitude, and comfort the heart in the hour of affliction; if, by inftilling the love of virtue, they elevate the mind to patriotic fentiments: then muft their votaries not be accounted ufelefs members of fociety. Then may they contemn the railings of ignorance and prejudice, and expect the efteem of every liberal mind. From an enlightened government they have a right to protection: from pofterity they may promife themfelves that fame which they deferve.

DISCOURSE

DISCOURSE

DELIVERED IN THE SWEDISH ACADEMY,

BY

N. L. SIÖBERG,

ON HIS ADMISSION, THE 13TH MAY, 1787.

DISCOURSE,

BY N. L. SIÖBERG.

GENTLEMEN,

HE whom you have condefcended to honour with a feat in this fociety, confecrated to merit, and to talents, has not the advantage to poffefs that warm and profound fagacity, nor that animating eloquence, which diftinguifhes genius. Nature has limited his faculties to a mere admiration of external and intellectual beauty, of ufeful and exalted talents. This is all, perhaps, that will be found in the few lines which he has written, and of which fome have been fo fortunate as to attract your notice, and to obtain your approbation.

How much will he, who formerly regarded not himself as one of the favourites of fortune, be stimulated in the career of letters, by the honour of an admission into a society, composed, as this is, of men the most distinguished for genius and abilities, which the Swedish nation can boast! He will certainly regret no longer the time which he has consumed in the cultivation of polite learning.

Permit me, Gentlemen, on this occasion, to recall to your memory some of those illustrious characters, by whom genius may be said to have been introduced into the world.

There have been nations more ancient than the Greeks, who possessed science; but, to the boast of genius, no people can establish a prior claim.

Homer is the greatest prodigy in the reign of genius. In no man did the poetic fire burn with equal constancy. In other writers the flame of genius is only visible by intervals. The major part of even their most masterly compositions, is filled with the play of words, with quaint points, with all those inferior graces, which can never reach the sublimity of genius; but those ebullitions of a poetic fancy, which agitated other authors in the composition of their best works, appear, in the breast of Homer, to have operated as an uniform principle. If this be true, he was the most fortunate of men. In other writers it is too visible, that the soul, which animates their works, is not that principle which actuates

the

the whole of their conduct. It is only by extraordinary efforts, that they can be elevated above their daily sphere of action. The cause of this is obvious. Conversation with other men is, at present, the principal object of all our studies. In order to please the multitude, we must resemble them; and in the efforts of a vulgar ambition, the fire of genius will consequently be extinguished. There is reason to believe, that HOMER, ever transported beyond himself, or removed from the circle of common life, had very little intercourse with his contemporaries. His two poems, the noblest monuments of human genius, appear to have been written, from first to last, without effort, as if they had been dictated by some superior intelligence. There is reason to believe, that they would have appeared, even had the human understanding never been able to comprehend them. HOMER seems to have appeared on the stage of existence, to produce the Iliad and the Odyssey, and then to expire.

A NATION, which had HOMER for the founder of its literature, might have been expected to have been favoured by the perpetual residence of the Muses, did not the continual fluctuation of human affairs, did not the destructive ambition of the spirit of war, forbid the hopes of immortality to all the works of man.

ALL the geniuses of Greece discover, in their productions, some shade of the Homerian pencil. Those of the first order exhibit the boldness of his invention, the sublimity of his outlines, the fertility of his imagination, and that noble contempt of insipid accuracy which distinguishes his works; those of the second order discover the simplicity of his style, the graces of his narration, and his skill in giving interest to the most familiar scenes of nature, and to the most common events of human life.

Some heaven-favoured writers we have seen, whom nature had placed next in degree to that immortal bard; they had the courage to enter the lists with him, they tried their force, they failed, they committed to the flames their verses, and were content to transfuse into prose the soul of their great master. Hence the source of eloquence.

The language which Homer employed, acquired under his plastic hands, almost all the powers and grace of which it was susceptible; it became the richest, the most sonorous, the most picturesque, the most majestic, that ever was uttered by mortal man.

The happy direction which Homer gave to the genius of the Greeks, remained unaltered till the destruction of their empire. Never did any other nation unite qualities so opposite: To a courage which was invincible in dangers, an inflexibility of determination, not to be shaken by adversity; they united the most ardent susceptibility of pleasure, and the most refined taste for voluptuous enjoyment; to the keen subtilty of logic, they added the most profound penetration; a florid imagination was accompanied by the most engaging simplicity of style. To the most extensive designs, and comprehensive views, they joined that spirit of discrimination which descends to the minuter graces. They had all that amiable vivacity which

enlivens

enlivens converſation, without that inſupportable vanity which generally attends it; nor, amongſt them, was that ſpirit of liberty and independance, which ariſes from a ſentiment of conſcious merit, disfigured by that ſeverity and pertinacity of opinion, to which it is too often attached.

But where now are thoſe heroes who ſubdued? Where now are thoſe ſages who enlightened the world? Why have a people diſappeared, who poſſeſſed within themſelves all thoſe great qualities which might have been expected to have eternized their empire? Unhappy Greece! thy melancholy lot ſhould ſtrike with terror every nation of the globe! What force, what talents, were like yours adapted to brave the efforts of all-deſtroying time? Ignorance, barbariſm, and ſlavery, now occupy that ſoil which was once the abode of genius, of liberty, and of heroiſm. Under theſe ſuperb, but now deſolated, porticoes, which once were the reſort of the poet, who was meditating a new Iliad; of the philoſopher, who was engaged in a new ſyſtem of the world; of the hero, who was concerting the deſtruction of the Perſian monarchy; now, alas! wanders the ignorant and lazy ALBANESE, regardleſs of the ſacred ruins that ſurround him, and only ſolicitous to eſcape the ravages of famine, and the fury of the ſword. The fountain of Caſtalia, once honoured by the viſit of Apollo and the Graces, no longer profuſely beſtows thoſe celeſtial tranſports, which ancient bards quaffed from that unſullied ſource. A ſcanty ſtream that oozes muddy from the ground, is all that it now yields to quench the thirſt of the barbarous inhabitant. Parnaſſus, where, armed with thunder,

Jove

Jove descended to shake the world, is now the retreat of wild beasts; and the distinguished spring, Helicon, is itself covered with thorns.

Since, however, it was ordained by fate, that Greece should experience a master, it was still, in some degree, fortunate for that country to pass under the yoke of Rome. Had the Carthaginians, or the Numidians, subjugated the Greeks, the barbarian victors would have burned their writings, destroyed their monuments, proscribed their sages; the genius and wisdom of Greece would have been overwhelmed in general ruin, and consigned to everlasting oblivion. From how slender a thread is sometimes suspended the fate of the universe! Had the Carthaginians vanquished the Romans, polished and lettered Europe the Mistress of the World, might have been at this day as vile and barbarous, as Negroland itself.

The Romans made themselves masters of the literature of the Greeks, no less than of their empire. VIRGIL, HORACE, OVID, immortal names! propagated the glory of LATIUM, farther than the victories of CÆSAR, of SCIPIO, of PAULUS EMILIUS had been able to pervade. But after the reign of AUGUSTUS, a set of monsters filled the Roman throne. From their cruel aspect, the Muses fled. Amidst those tyrants, however, arose the scourge of tyranny, the immortal TACITUS. He is one of those men, in whom indignation was the parent of genius. He lived in the midst of those human butchers, and he would have been their victim, had they possessed sufficient penetration to recognize the

man,

man, who was deftined to immortalize their infamy. Fate had placed him in a fituation peculiarly advantageous to the exertions of his talents. On every fide the moft hideous vices, and the moft fublime virtues, provoked the burning energy of his pen. The Roman empire was convulfed by the alternate ftruggles of freedom and of flavery. The minds of men had begun to recover from that confternation, into which they had been thrown by the victories of CÆSAR, and the policy of AUGUSTUS. The greater part had degenerated, not only from the dignity of freedom, but were even degraded below the level of flavery itfelf: but in fome bofoms the Roman fpirit burned with unabated fire. Thefe oppofite difpofitions exhibited a ftriking contraft; but an inftructive fpectacle to a mind like that of TACITUS. Hence he learned to appreciate man in all his various relations of public or private life. His works cannot be denominated hiftory. But that form appeared to him the beft adapted to collect, in a body, his profound obfervations on the human mind; the labour of many years. He wrote a thoufand years ago, and yet, with all our philofophy, with all our moral difcoveries, we cannot boaft of having carried farther than him the knowledge of human nature. He muft have poffeffed almoft fupernatural fagacity to anticipate, as he has done, the experience of ages. The reflections of TACITUS contain the germ of a new fyftem of ethics, as well as of legiflation. To underftand TACITUS, a certain portion of genius is required. MACHIAVEL, GRATIAN, LA ROCHEFOUCAULT, MONTESQUIEU, HELVETIUS, are writers whom he has created. Although he did not affume the pen to flatter by happy turns and pleafing images the apathy of the human race, whom,

perhaps,

perhaps, he defpifed; yet there exifts not a writer fo interefting. Did a man embrace in his memory the literature of the whole world, ftill would TACITUS be new to him. Without obfcurity, natural or ftudied, he affords his readers the grateful pleafure of paufing at every phrafe to difcover his meaning. But it is only in his native tongue, that we can prove this pleafure. All the modern languages of Europe are too methodical in their movements, and too ftrictly limited in the meaning of their words, to admit his poignant equivoque. TACITUS offers almoft as many thoughts as words. It is this laconic and concife ftyle which his difciples, the great and immortal authors whom I have juft mentioned, have imitated. But they have alfo imbibed a portion of his fpirit; they have dared to utter grand and extraordinary truths: but the light of truth is yet too refplendent; our eyes are ftill too weak to bear her luftre.

THE remembrance of victories vanifhes with the difafters which they occafioned; fyftems of philofophy inceffantly fucceed each other, and fall in their turn: but the mafter-pieces of polite learning remain, becaufe the emotions of the heart, and the fportivenefs of the imagination, are eternally the fame. O, Rome! time has, indeed, fapped thy threatning walls, fire has devoured thy extenfive palaces; thy magnificent ftatues have mingled with the duft; thy formidable armies, like thin vapours, have difappeared, and the pomp of thy triumphs have left only an empty noife in the world: but the immortal labours of thy genius have braved the ravages of time, the force of flames, the fury of bar-

barians,

barians, and still survive in spite of the uncertainty of human glory.

The Barbarians could not destroy the influence of the Italian climate, which inspires a taste for polite literature, and a tenderness of soul. But I pass over the ages of ignorance, and direct my hasty steps to thee, O Tasso, poet sublime and picturesque! In whose life we see the model of what most men of genius are fated to undergo. The profound, impetuous, and eternal flame of love which consumed thee, thy imagination ever active which still impelled thee to objects unknown, to new creations; the inveterate persecution of fate, the obstinacy of thy countrymen in refusing to acknowledge thy merit, and in fine, after the melancholy period of thy days, thy name increasing in fame, and spreading wide in glory; every circumstance of thy life, in short, proves thee a genuine votary of the God of genius.

Tasso gave to the Italian language an energy, of which from its softness it did not seem susceptible; and to poetry an elevation, which the then predominating quaintness of style appeared to counteract. That tender and plaintive tone, that taste for magnificence, that luxuriance of brilliant images, and that predilection for fairy scenery which distinguish the Italian poetry, were introduced by Tasso.

In our days Italy produced a man of the first rank in the empire of genius *, but death interrupted him in his career of fame perhaps before his genius was completely mature. Sweden possesses his ashes, and our language preserves a portion of his genius. He admired our King, he loved our country. Educated in the language of the most artificial softness in Europe, he delighted in the simple graces of our tongue. He has enriched our literature with two excellent morsels of eloquence.

The literature of France has the reputation of possessing the most classical taste, and the advantage of the most general reception. RACINE, the greatest genius of that country, had the art of rendering himself agreeable to every class of readers, and is become the literary legislator of his nation. The genius of RACINE is truly French. It would be difficult to succeed in France with a genius different from his. Few men have written with the grace, the purity, the harmony which ennoble the writings of this author. He who is not charmed with his composition, is an alien to the Muses. He never overcharges the passions, never forces them beyond the bounds which nature has prescribed; he is ever noble, ever true. He is an eminent example of the force, the grace, the sublimity of which the genuine feelings of the heart are susceptible.

* The Abbè MICHELESSI, who died at Stokholm in 1773.

RACINE

RACINE determined the ſtructure of the French language. He endowed it with regularity, harmony, purity, and neatneſs of expreſſion.

In the flowery paths of letters, FONTAINE is the legiſlator of France. There he has never been ſurpaſſed, never indeed equalled by any writer. Literature is naturally divided into two kinds, the ſerious, and the gay. In the latter there are but few degrees of perfection. He who has not attained the moſt eminent, may be ſaid to have done nothing. In this ſpecies of writing a man is born with all the excellence he can ever attain. The deſire of elevation would be an impediment to his ſucceſs. To excel in this line of compoſition, a man muſt abſolutely have no other purſuit. He whoſe heart is but ſlightly touched by any paſſion, he who pants for fame, or who permits the cares of this world to trouble his repoſe, will never become a FONTAINE. This writer conſidered himſelf as placed upon the earth merely to reſpire the breath of life, and to ſport the happy ſallies which occurred to him in his careleſs progreſs through the world. The leaſt informed characters might have converſed with him all his life without ſuffering his deriſion, and the wittieſt of mortals would not have excited his admiration. He was wholly unconſcious of his powers. Never could he be perſuaded to think himſelf of any weight in the world of letters. His works coſt him nothing. Hence he regarded them as trifles, and believed, with the greateſt ſimplicity, that others did ſo too. He treated as a ſally of extravagance and folly, the aſſertion of a perſon, who preferred his fables to thoſe of Æſop and of Phædrus. Such a man was very far from ſuſpecting, that his writings

writings were the glory of French literature, and that his name was an honour to his country.

FONTAINE is the confolation of thofe, who have not the gift of invention. He has proved that without it a perfon may in a certain degree be a great genius. He has furpaffed thofe who invented the fubjects of his pen.

FONTAINE has endowed the French language with the graces of an engaging fimplicity and amiable gaiety, which no tongue ancient or modern has in an equal degree obtained.

AMONGST the fucceffors of RACINE fome have nearly approached his pitch of excellence: but FONTAINE remains unrivalled.

THE author who difplays the greateft energy in the French language, is certainly JEAN-JACQUES ROUSSEAU, the moft moving, the moft eloquent of all writers. This man alone gives a fuperiority to the prefent age above all that have preceded. He who feels the inftinct of genius, will thank his deftiny for delaying his birth till the period that produced JEAN-JACQUES. He was one of thofe men, whom Providence fends at different periods among the human race, to fupport the dignity of their nature. Happy it is for humanity, that a man of his extraordinary powers has confecrated his eloquence to the caufe of virtue. Arrayed in the charms of his enchanting ftyle, fhe can never henceforward become the object of derifion

rifion or contempt. If a man should suddenly become immoral, if he should break all the bonds of society, to center his whole existence in mere self, still he could never become insensible to the force of ROUSSEAU's genius, nor elude the fascination of his eloquence. He had in view in his works a more sublime object, than any preceding philosopher: which was to reconduct man to his primitive simplicity of manners. But so far removed from that happy state did he find the human race, that several years spent in painful researches, could scarce enable him to discover the man of nature. He conceived him happy and amiable, and lamented that the efforts of a hundred ages had only served to remove him farther and farther from the path of felicity.

THE language of Rousseau will ever be the predominant language of Europe. Other languages may excel it in point of force, or of harmony, of flexibility or copiousness, but still they will never be the language of JEAN-JACQUES. To the most uncultivated language ROUSSEAU would have given celebrity. It is with languages, as it is with geniuses; the most luminious may remain concealed for want of a skillful hand to introduce them into light.

ROUSSEAU has the admirable art of stealing into the bosom of his readers. He appears to have studied the disposition of every individual. He who seeks only for solidity of reasoning, will find it in ROUSSEAU: he who reads merely to be amused, will be fascinated by his style. The moralist regards him as the apostle of virtue: and the decent disciple

ciple of Epicurus has him ever in his hand. He resembles the rainbow which, according to Newton, varies its colours with the varying optics of different spectators.

Of all authors Rousseau is the greatest favourite of the ladies: a proof that the most sublime flights of genius are not above their capacity, provided the author neglects not to sacrifice to the graces. The fair sex delight in the writings of Rousseau; because, for the honour of nature, he is of all the learned the least ostentatious of erudition.

In casting a slight glance on the literature of England, we are struck with astonishment at the croud of geniuses which appear. It seems like traversing ancient Rome, where, at each step we encounter some great man, some conqueror of a powerful nation, or some venerable patriot, who has rejected with disdain a foreign crown, to remain a simple citizen at home. The English have certainly very little desire to propagate their literature beyond the limits of their own country. They resemble those states, by whose fundamental laws the spirit of conquest is proscribed. But at home their power is formidable indeed. An English writer, who should be regarded with veneration by all Europe, but whom his countrymen considered with indifference, would lament the obscurity of his name. What has been said of the Romans, that they were an assemblage of heroes, may, in a literature sense be applied to the English; the whole nation bears the impression of genius.

I SHALL content myself with only mentioning two of their great authors. MILTON composed a poem so energetic, so sublime, that, on its first appearance, it was superior to the conception even of the English themselves. In the present age, which has done justice to almost every instance of neglected merit, the English are delighted to find that their country and their language possesses one of the most sublime productions of the human mind. In MILTON nature had reversed her wonted order of proceeding. In youth he was a politician, in old age he was a poet. MILTON astonishes the judgment of his readers. All the rules of poetic probability disappear before him. As we read, we are wholly immersed in admiration. But, if instead of genius, the reader possesses a geometrical exactness only, and if he has substituted to sensibility a factitious taste, he will pause to criticise MILTON at every line. In fact, it would be highly absurd to expect in works of imagination a mathematical correctness. We are organised to feel rather than to think. Nature therefore has given us but few channels of intelligence; but those of sensation she has multiplied without end. Of regularity she is not ambitious. She has never promised to defend us from deception. On the contrary, her most beautiful phenomena are splendid illusions; and the most enchanting pleasures of life only delightful chimeras.

POPE was actuated by a continual energy of genius. Philosophy and the graces seem to have vied with each other in forming him to deliver through a new channel, truths the most important and energetic to the human race. Poetry which hitherto had flattered the ear, and bloomed only

only to the imagination, became in his hands the tutoress of man, whom she conducted by charms till then unknown, to a knowledge of his various relations to himself, to the univerſe, and to his author. So brilliant was the merit of POPE, that even in his life-time he triumphed over an hoſt of literary banditti, who dared to conſpire againſt his fame. But we, nations of the continent, are ignorant of their writings, nor have their odious names ever paſſed the limits of their iſle. POPE exhibited to Europe HOMER, ſublime, ſonorous, and majeſtic, as when he charmed the ancient Greeks. If the rage of depreſſing modern merit were not natural to the human race, the tranſlator of HOMER would have ſeen a temple erected to his honour.

MILTON and POPE have carried the Engliſh language to a ſtate of perfection, which no modern language can equal.

IN every nation there are two paths to glory: literature, and arms. One half of Europe our arms have ſubjugated, and made the other tremble. To convert Swedes into heroes, is no difficult taſk. Nature, in that reſpect, has been bountiful of materials. But becauſe they abound in valour, is it therefore fair to refuſe them genius? The ſame ardour of ſoul, which, in the field of battle, inſpires a contempt of danger, will alſo, in ſolitude, inflame the poet, and exalt the genius to thoſe ſublime flights, which raiſe the admiration of the world. A coward is as incapable of genius as of heroiſm.

BEYOND

Beyond the imperfect glory of military virtue, the greatest of our Monarchs have never been able to conduct the nation. For GUSTAVUS the III. it was reserved to complete the glory of the Swedish name. By the powerful incitements of example and encouragement he has in a few years effected, that which many generations of worthy sovereigns were not able to accomplish. The literary glory of Sweden he has created; and rescued from oblivion her military honours *. The trophies of victory vanish and are forgotten, except the voice of genius proclaim the warlike exploits; nor from the silent tomb will the influence of the hero far extend; nor will many be excited to the imitation of his great or patriotic exertions, unless the glowing pencil of Eloquence emblazon them in the Temple of Fame.

In the present age the human mind appears to be more alert and restless than in any of the preceding. The rage of war, and the frenzy of fanaticism were the only passions that, at different periods, broke in upon the lethargy of our ancestors. When these two powerful springs of human action began to relax, some other aliment was sought for to feed the incessant cravings of the human heart. Long had philosophy, long had polite literature, ethics, and the fine arts, invited us in vain to their charming retreats: at length we pursue them

---

* He has not only rescued from oblivion the memory of the ancient military honours of Sweden, but has renovated, and may be said to have created, the martial glory of the nation, which had been eclipsed for upwards of a century. The naval victory of Swenskfund, which terminated the war of 1788, is the most complete conquest that ever graced the arms of any people, and the first which the Swedes have obtained since 1712.

with avidity. Let those who govern the nations learn, as those who are blessed with genius must feel, that the human race will in the end obtain, by means of the arts, that tranquillity after which they have so long and so vainly aspired.

In you, Gentlemen, I behold the agents of this inestimable advantage: philosophy, politics, oratory, poesy, have no treasures of which some of you are not masters. Moulded by your skilful hands, our language recedes more and more from its ancient rudeness. We have seen it bend to the subtile graces of the most refined raillery, we have examples of its following the tempestuous career of passion, and soaring to the most sublime flights of imagination. As with ornaments, it is with languages; they are becoming only on beautiful objects.

DISCOURSE

DELIVERED IN THE SWEDISH ACADEMY,

BY THE SENATOR

COUNT T. G. OXENSTIERNA,

PRESIDENT TO THE GRAND COUNCIL OF THE ROYAL CHANCERY, FIRST LORD OF THE BEDCHAMBER TO HIS MAJESTY, GRAND MASTER OF HER MAJESTY'S HOUSEHOLD, COMMANDER OF THE ORDER OF THE POLAR STAR;

On his Admiſſion, March 20, 1786.

DISCOURSE

BY

COUNT T. G. OXENSTIERNA,

GENTLEMEN,

IF a warm attachment to purfuits, to which this Academy is devoted, were a qualification fufficient for becoming a member of it, no one perhaps would have a ftronger claim than myfelf to a place in this affembly. Wholly engroffed by the happinefs of fuch a fituation, I fhould feel a pleafure, which the comparifon of my own defects with your diftinguifhed talents, would be unable to difturb. In the contemplation of my unmerited good fortune, I fhould be fometimes diverted from reflection upon the diftance, which feparates your productions from the trifles which, though they have ferved occafionally to amufe a vacant hour, were little calculated to attract the public attention.

DESTITUTE as I am of every talent which, by securing your approbation, is certain to secure a seat at your illustrious board; I am nevertheless impressed with the most lively sense of the eminent service which a Monarch, dear to our hearts, has done to the cause of polite literature, by fixing upon you, Gentlemen, as the proper instruments for raising it to perfection. Incapable of affording any example in myself, I have the singular felicity, of being numbered in the society of such, as are most amply endowed with every requisite, to make them models of excellence. Charmed with the prospect, my fancy anticipates the height, to which those soaring geniuses will attain, who, following the light of your instructions, will hereafter exalt the reputation of our literature by a purity of diction, added to elevation, and energy of thought. Already, invigorated by your precepts, poetry prepares to transmit to posterity, in the most brilliant and glowing colours, a picture of the opinions and polished manners of an enlightened age. Already solicitous to immortalize in the language of our country the memory of its great men, eloquence discovers in the persons of those, who have enriched her with the choicest ornaments of speech, the most deserving objects of her praise. With admiration I contemplate the protector of the belles lettres condescending to enrol his illustrious name with the names of those whom he has directed to promulgate and maintain the rules which genius avows, and of which his own is an eminent example.

THIS code, seconded and supported by his example, will finally settle and decide the opinions of a reflecting age, which no longer regards the study of polite literature as tending to cast a damp upon the martial spirit of a manly people. The country which has given birth to heroes, now delights to deck with literary laurels the warrior brow; and in the fine arts, so often accused of enervating the mind, sees only that mild influence which, by smoothing the ruggedness of virtue, gives her charms which the Graces alone can bestow. Cloathed in the resplendent robes of genius, and invested with the magnificent grandeur of history, Virtue will henceforward present herself to a people, whose veneration shall amply compensate her past oppression. Her future triumph is secured; and by poetry and eloquence transmitted to after ages, the memory of her immortal actions shall brighten to the admiring view of far remote posterity.

AWAKENED by the dawn of the age of GUSTAVUS from a long night of torpidity, the Swedish Muses find here a peaceful asylum. Charmed with inhabiting a temple, which he has dedicated to their service, happy in assembling at the cheerful call of a genius, who animates them by his example no less than his munificence, they repair towards the North in a garb far more becoming, than when, following the footsteps of our ancient warriors, they engraved on the rude tombs of pirates the Runic praise. Now their only difficulty is to select an object from the multitude of heroes who press forward to immortality; while at the foot of that throne, where formerly, in rude

and

and diffonant notes, they fang favage fcenes of flaughter and devaftation, they now celebrate the ferenity of concord, the bleffings of liberty, and the love of the human race.

WITH ungrateful filence the Mufes have never been reproached. Never have they abandoned to oblivion the memory of their benefactors. It is not now for the firft time, that the heir to the fceptre of the VASA's, receives the homage of their adoration. The glory of his anceftors adorns their annals, a glory, which they are ever ready to vindicate as their own. To their now protector they now approach with the fame tribute of love and veneration, which to the name of GUSTAVUS they have ever willingly offered up. With alacrity they difcharge the duty, which Fame commits to their care; and eager to paint the fublimeft virtues, they quit the fictions of antiquity, to prefent to the world in colours, tempered by Genius and the Graces, a picture drawn by the hand of truth.

THE END.

www.ingramcontent.com/pod-product-compliance
Lightning Source LLC
Chambersburg PA
CBHW020151170426
43199CB00010B/989